Jesus Breaks the Chain of Offense

Diane Bernardin

TRILOGY CHRISTIAN PUBLISHERS

TUSTIN, CA

Trilogy Christian Publishers
A Wholly Owned Subsidary of Trinity Broadcasting Network
2442 Michelle Drive
Tustin, CA 92780

Jesus Breaks the Chain of Offense

Rights Department, 2442 Michelle Drive, Tustin, CA 92780.

Trilogy Christian Publishing/TBN and colophon are trademarks of Trinity Broadcasting Network.

Book Cover & Abuse Artwork Painted by Pepsi Freund

For information about special discounts for bulk purchases, please contact Trilogy Christian Publishing.

Trilogy Disclaimer: The views and content expressed in this book are those of the author and may not necessarily reflect the views and doctrine of Trilogy Christian Publishing or the Trinity Broadcasting Network.

Manufactured in the United States of America

10 9 8 7 6 5 4 3 2 1

Library of Congress Cataloging-in-Publication Data is available.

ISBN: 978-1-68556-016-4

E-ISBN: 978-1-68556-017-1

Contents

Dedication

I would like to dedicate this book to every individual who has ever received an offense. Because I know the turmoil of what offenses bring to one's soul, I am offering the way of escape given to me by my Lord and Savior, Jesus Christ.

I also dedicate this book to my Lord and Savior Jesus Christ, to His wonderful Father, and to His precious Holy Spirit, who responded to a crying heart that wanted freedom, no matter what it took. Psalm 34:19 says, *"Many are the afflictions of the righteous, but the Lord delivers them out of them all."* Thank You, Lord, that You have made me a living testimony that Your word works. I am forever grateful!

"To get to the blackberries, you have to go through the thorns and you'll shed blood."

Michel Bernardin

Acknowledgements

I want to first and foremost thank my Lord and Savior, Jesus Christ, for allowing this revelation to come through this clay vessel and for bringing salvation and deliverance to all those who call upon His wonderful name. I want to thank my loving husband, Michel, for his patience with me and for supporting me with encouragement in the release of this book.

Also, my two beautiful daughters, Jacqueline and Jennifer, who have blessed me as a grandmother with three of the most beautiful offspring; I am so fortunate! I want to thank my precious mentor and spiritual mother, Theresa Duffy, who has encouraged me by spending countless hours strengthening my inner man and changing my thinking. Where there was error, Theresa provided instruction and emanated the love of Christ. She is truly a priceless treasure, and I am privileged to know her.

I want to thank my dear friend, Pepsi Freund, who most graciously and efficiently assisted with the writing and, overall, everything of this book. The love for this sister goes unsaid. Her sense of humor carried us both through this one! I want to thank my Christian, caring, and generous employer, Pat Thiessen, who allowed me to write this book on her company time with permission. Words cannot express how grateful I am, and I pray a multiplied harvest to her in return.

I want to thank my precious sister, Sharon Varchetto, my prayer buddy and great encourager who spent countless hours praying with me over many things, never once complaining. I will always be grateful to have such a prayer warrior for a sister; I am truly a blessed woman.

"The ultimate measure of a man [or woman] is not where he [or she] stands in moments of comfort and convenience, but where he [or she] stands at times of challenge and controversy."

Martin Luther King, Jr.

Foreword

"I will not receive an offense from anybody, at any time, for any reason!" Diane, together with the congregation at the Rock of Sarasota, has quoted that statement in unison, more times than she or they will ever remember. Now, through the wonderful healing she herself has received over the years, she has been gifted by God with the keys to unlock the truths of how to possess what they have confessed.

Glory to His wonderful name! This powerful statement that has rolled from their lips on so many occasions was a mandate His Majesty placed upon me more than eleven years ago. And now, together with the powerful "set free" anointing of the Holy Spirit and with the advent of this "know-how" manual for victory, those who are trapped by this deadly adversary will be guided safely to the shores of a healthy, dynamic Christian life.

I strongly urge you to take the time out of your busy schedule and ask God to illuminate your understanding, that you may fully grasp the simple yet powerful truths illustrated herein as you receive the wisdom contained in the pages of this book.

Diane is a walking case study of how vividly and unmistakably reliable the truths are to the everyday individual that will embrace and walk out what they read on these pages. May God richly bless you as you begin your journey to wholeness.

In His service,

Richard L. Brantley
Senior Pastor/Rock of Sarasota
Sarasota, Florida

"Forgiveness is unlocking the door to set someone free and realizing you were the prisoner..."

Unknown

Introduction

Offenses are one of the most effective hidden strategies of the kingdom of darkness used to paralyze the church today. Jesus said while referring to the signs of His glorious return to the earth, "And then many will be offended, will betray one another, and will hate one another" (Matthew 24:10). It does not take a rocket scientist to see that the world has turned cold toward one another.

There was a day that we never had to lock our front doors, windows, or cars. Business deals were made complete with the shaking of hands or the promise of a word. Today, if it isn't in writing, it doesn't hold worth, and some of us have to barbwire our fences, bar our windows from thieves, and invest in expensive alarm systems for security. There is very little trust today, regrettably even in the church.

With the increase of fallen ministries, exposure of political figures, the increase in crimes like terrorism, offenses are on the rise everywhere. The good news is

Jesus is well aware of all. Proverbs 15:3 says, *"The eyes of the Lord are in every place keeping watch on the evil and the good."*

I received this beautiful email sent to me a few years ago, and I know it will bring comfort to your soul as it did mine.

"Before the beginning of time, I planned it this way... to dwell in you, walk in you. Be your God and call you My own. What you go through, I go through. I'm not just near you but in you. I'm not just here in the nick of time, but all the time. I'm here leading, guiding, strengthening, healing, coaching, encouraging, warning, protecting...and most importantly, loving you. My desire is to have an intimate relationship with you and for you to have intimate knowledge of My love and anointing and be filled with My fullness. Rest in My love. Act in My love. I will do exceeding abundant above all that you ask or think, according to My power that works in you.

"Your loving heavenly Father"

"We are all pencils in the hand of a writing God, who is sending love letters to the world."

Mother Theresa

CHAPTER 1

What is an Offense?

Most of us know what an offense is; at least, we think we do. A good definition for the word "offense" is "a snare or a trap; something that outrages the moral or physical senses." So, we can conclude that an offense is a snare or trap set up that causes outrage in our moral senses. Who sets up these traps for us? The Lord or Satan? The answer is Satan. Offense is a spirit assigned by Satan strategically to bring division to the church, to families, and relationships to bring them to a paralyzed state so they do nothing for God. If the enemy of our soul can cause the people of God to turn on each other, then they will not unite to accomplish anything for the kingdom of God. The word of God spoken by Jesus to the Pharisees throughout the New Testament brought an offense to them.

They became enraged with Him because He stated the truth about His identity, His Father, and His kingdom. Why did the greatest attacks against the ministry of Jesus come from the religious leaders? This spirit of offense, as well as many other spirits sent from Satan himself, possessed these religious leaders to plot our Lord's death, seeking to trap Him and stop Him from doing the work of His Father. It became a relentless obsession with them, but remember Jesus willingly laid down His life for our sake. Here they had the Son of Almighty God standing right in front of them, and they could not perceive it.

They claimed to know God and stood in fancy robes in the marketplace to be seen by others all around them and speak how wonderful they were. When Jesus (the light of the world) showed up, everything that was hidden in their hearts was exposed. We have the same offenses today in this world around us. The walls of division are set up everywhere in the name of God, G_D, Allah, and the list goes on. The true followers of Jesus Christ have suffered persecution, violence, ridicule, and death for their belief. Why would the enemy seek so diligently to silence those who declare their testimony of the lordship of Jesus Christ? What is the enemy so afraid of that he would need to silence them? Hint: Truth; you see, if you are not walking in the truth, you are not a threat to the enemy at all. If the truth is exposed, you will become a strategic assignment to be silenced.

Truth stirs up the dark kingdom because the word says in John 8:32, *"And you shall know the truth, and the truth shall make you free."* I believe the main reason behind church splits is due to offenses that entered in and were never resolved. The word states in Ephesians 6:12, *"For we do not wrestle against flesh and blood, but against principalities, against powers, against the rulers of the darkness of this age, against spiritual hosts of wickedness in heavenly places."* This clearly states who the real enemy is: Satan and the demonic forces working with him. As long as the spirits that operate in our lives remain hidden, they have an unseen power. Only when they are exposed and the church learns how to defeat them will there be unity restored in the body of Christ. I cannot keep silent when I know the freedom I received can be transferred to others. For this reason alone, I write this book to help those who are caught in this deadly trap as I was.

The journey may be painful, but the fruit from your obedience will be well worth it. Jesus is coming back for a bride without spot or wrinkle, and this is a process in which our consent is required and our wills are surrendered to His. There is a price for obtaining toward this "mark" of the high calling in Christ, but when we draw closer, I assure you there is no desire to ever turn back! There may be pain that rises up within you as you read as you recall those old hurts that were not ever dealt with, but this is only a tool in the hands of our Maker to reach way down inside your heart to make you whole again so that His beauty may be seen upon you everywhere you go, so let that pain come forth, and the gold that is hidden beneath will shine!

"When you suffer and lose, that does not mean you are being disobedient to God. In fact, it might mean you're right in the center of His will. The path of obedience is often marked by times of suffering and loss."

Charles (Chuck) Swindoll

CHAPTER 2

Recognize an Offense

In order to help you come out of an offense attack, you must first recognize it when it comes your way. Jesus said in Matthew 18:7, *"Woe to the world because of offenses! For offenses must come, but woe to that man by whom the offense comes!"* So, we see that offenses will come our way; there is nothing we can do to prevent them from being launched against us. The most common way for this spirit of offense to attack is in the form of words, but it can operate simply through body language. These attacks never come at an expected time, nor are we prepared to receive them. The enemy sees to that, as he is a military strategist and operates through deception. This spirit desires to stay hidden in or around you, so it has a continuous open door to come and go any time it wills to damage your soul. When offensive words are spoken through the offender, an invisible missile is launched by the enemy into the mind or soul of the individual. You who have been offended can literally feel it penetrate your heart like a sword.

The enemy has no mercy and loves to sneak this attack upon you and catch you off guard. The worst kind of offense is an unjust, undeserved, or untruthful one. That is where Satan earned his name, the accuser of the brethren. Jesus would never attack His people this way. He confronts with truth, a big difference. He confronted the religious leaders and exposed who they were serving and all the sin and darkness hidden in their hearts. The truth is an offense to the devil as well as the cross of Jesus Christ because truth and the cross defeated Satan two thousand years ago. The fruit of every offense is immediate rejection.

Then come the tapes that are sent across the mind of the offended, "I cannot believe they just said that or this just happened. Did you hear what they just said to you? Are you going to put up with this?" These tapes will play over and over again; then, you will feel anger rising toward that person. (Of course, not knowing the person was just used by the enemy.) I then would rehearse the words I would like to respond to that person, and they are not kind, but I was not a confronter. Now, at this point, most people decide they will never talk to that person again, never want to see them again as long as they live, and quietly leave their presence with a wounded, damaged heart. There is no trust in that person any longer. The verdict is decided: Done with that one! Those wounds not dealt with create an open door for the spirit to come and go as Satan's worker declares, "Job done." Proverbs 18:19 says, *"A brother offended is harder to win than a strong city. And contentions are like the bars of a castle."* Every offense you receive becomes a brick, and before long, a wall is constructed. You then become filled with strife and isolate yourself in order to prevent any future wounds or rejections.

You become a strong city when those bricks are piled high. Romans 14:17 says, *"For the kingdom of God is not eating and drinking, but righteousness and peace and joy in the Holy Spirit."* These are the fruits of the kingdom of God operating in you as a believer. This is what the Holy Spirit produces in the believer's heart as they submit themselves completely over to His rule and reign in their lives. The Holy Spirit will restore your soul with joy and peace when you pray and ask Him for help. I have not found one offended person who is filled with righteousness (right standing with God), peace, or the joy of the Holy Spirit. The fruit is blocked from operating like a huge boulder dropped inside your spiritual well. That is exactly its purpose, to stop the flow of living water flowing from you to others. That living water brings salvation to the lost. You must choose whether you will hold onto that boulder that weighs you down or do something to destroy it completely.

Right now, you are probably thinking, *Diane, but you don't know what they did to me. My offense is justified. They deserve some sort of vengeance; after all, they hurt me for no reason!* Please, read on. *"It's not what you know, it's what you do with what you know."*

Unknown

CHAPTER 3

My Testimony

After much prayer and searching the word for truth, the Lord showed me where my offense story began. At age three, one of my brothers stole my dinner off my plate. Growing up in a very large family with four brothers and three sisters, my precious mother would cook for an army! One of my brothers liked to steal the food off the plate of those not paying attention. One time, when it was my turn, I caught on to this diabolical deed and became enraged at the injustice but was afraid to ever confront him as he was much older and stronger than me.

This produced fear, no safety, and no trust in anyone at such an early age. Fear ruled over my soul, and without knowing it, these spirits were tormenting me all the time. For anyone who is bound by a spirit of fear, they know all the torment that comes with it. There is good news, though; the word says in 2 Timothy 1:7, *"For God has not given us a spirit of fear, but of power and of love and of a sound mind."* That is the truth, so claim it now!

The offensive attacks increased as I attended school, and missiles were sent through classmates as well as teachers. Offense and its fruit, rejection, had full control over my life. I would isolate myself from others so they wouldn't hurt me anymore. I had very few friends because I had become what I hated most, an offender. I was never aware of it, nor did I know how to stop it. I had few friends because I couldn't trust anyone. I was a silent rebel as a teenager, and as a result, I was full of rage.

Why couldn't I have a family like the Brady Bunch (my made-up, perfect, fantasy family) that I thought represented a normal home? I decided (made an inner vow) that when I grew older, I would get away from everyone and live on my own happily ever after with no offenders to ever bother me again. At eleven years old, I had a dream about Jesus. I was in this huge dining room in what I believe to be a mansion, and it had the most beautiful dark wooden furniture; even the walls were a very expensive wood I had never seen anywhere here on earth. I heard my earthly dad's voice say, "Get your shoes on, kids, we're going for a ride."

I started walking around looking for some shoes when I saw this wooden elevator door open, and there stood Jesus in a white robe. He had shoulder-length brown hair and a dark beard, and if I had to estimate, He was about thirty years old and six feet tall. I wasn't concentrating on His face as I knew who He was. My eyes gazed at His shoes. I noticed He was wearing Roman sandals with the strings tied up around His calf. Oh, how I wanted His shoes! The next thing I knew, He disappeared but left those shoes on the elevator floor for me. I quickly put them on and ran for the front door. This mansion was located by a huge ocean, which I saw after opening the door. I jumped into a car with my family, and then I woke up. When I told my mother about this dream, she said maybe I would be a saint. Well, I was anything but a saint.

The offenses continued on, and destruction began to follow. Every job I had within a few months was lost, then my health, my reputation, friends, marriage, even my cat disappeared. Many times, thoughts of self-pity came, even wanting to leave these cruel people on earth, which is exactly what Satan hoped for. I felt like a real-life Job. Death was operating in every area of my life. On Thanksgiving night 1984, while I was celebrating with pink champagne, my sister Sharon came down for a visit. There was something so different about her; she had become a born-again Christian who stopped drinking and smoking and now was reading her Bible and talking about Jesus all the time. I was shocked, to say the least, and tried to talk her into truly celebrating the way she used to; after all, it was Thanksgiving.

While I was totally drunk, she led me to the Lord Jesus through the sinner's prayer. She said, "You've tried everything else in this world; why not give Jesus a try? He loves you!" Those wonderful words produced tears that continued for hours because she spoke words of truth. It was so hard for me to believe that Jesus would even look in my direction, let alone love me, but I knew something was very different about my sister, and she seemed so happy and at peace now. I wanted what she had. I woke up that next morning, and every desire for drinking had left me. It wasn't long after that I quit smoking with the Lord's help. I moved close to my sister and started attending her church, reading the Bible, and learned a lot about Jesus from her.

I wanted to know Jesus like she did. I began to attend her church and my, the hugs they gave to you, by total strangers! Those hugs were exactly what I needed. I was so grateful that the Jesus I heard about was a living Savior who truly loved me just the way I was. It wasn't long before we went out soul-winning for Jesus on the streets together. What an honor to be trusted by the King of kings to lead someone into His kingdom and pray for the sick. We saw Jesus perform many awesome miracles.

People were healed of cancer, paralysis, and back problems, to name a few. We grew so hungry for the presence of God and wanted to know the "secret" that these ministers had that allowed God to move through their life so greatly. So, we would travel for hours every weekend to go to those meetings where the anointing of God was present, and we left with such peace and joy. To experience His presence and anointing is a greater high than any drink or drug in the world could ever give, and you get no hangover! Although I was getting so blessed spiritually, I was struggling financially. I moved at least six times back and forth with my family because I couldn't make ends meet as a single mother. I couldn't understand why I was so prosperous in my spiritual growth but not financially.

As a matter of fact, I hadn't seen many blessings in my life, and I had to find out why. I did all the scriptural things to do that were taught. Tithes and offerings were above that, but I was always coming up short in the provision area. My pastor gave me a wonderful word regarding this. He said the Lord showed him a bucket, and it had a hole in the bottom of it. As quickly as the bucket filled with provision, the money was released through the hole. He said, "Diane, I know you are giving, but much of your giving is from emotional giving, instead of the Lord telling you where and how much to give. From now on, pray and ask the Lord before you give, and you'll see a change."

I saw some change, but I knew the Lord was pressing me to seek Him further regarding this, and it wouldn't leave me. I read this book with a checklist that named all the generational blessings and curses, and I was checking all the curses instead of the blessings. Here I was, a blood-bought covenant child of the living God, living on this earth as the black sheep of heaven. Seeking the Lord diligently for deliverance and answers, I got into every prayer line I could find, but still no results. Sharon and I were revival junkies and visited many of them. I begged the Lord continually (keep on knocking? I was banging!) for help. I would say, "Lord, if You would only show me what was repeatedly stealing from me, then I would repent of that sin right away." Crying, praying, fasting, even my plea bargaining with God never worked (so I thought).

Then one day, a close friend of mine introduced me to a woman from her church named Theresa. She would be the mentor the Lord allowed into my life to get me back on track. Theresa knew about deliverance, and the Lord used her mightily to break strongholds and generational curses off of my life. She was a mighty exhorter and saw me through the eyes of Jesus with unconditional love. As a spiritual mother, she told me what I needed to hear, not what I wanted to hear. I would exhort all who read this book to find spiritual mothers and fathers in your church who will nurture you and speak truth into your life by the spirit of the Lord. Then the Lord brought a spiritual father to me, Pastor Richard

Brantley. He, likewise, was so full of the love of Jesus, and the Lord's compassion flowed out of him like rivers. Spiritual mothers and fathers are so needed in the body of Christ and are divinely sent by God to mature the saints. Let the elders teach the younger in the Lord. So, if you are an elder saint, God may be calling upon you to train up the younger generation of saints and bring them to maturity. One day, during a time of intercessory prayer at my church, the Lord gave me an open vision. I saw Jesus standing at the front of the church next to this pit with flames of fire shooting out of it, covered by a metal grate. I saw the Lord pull off the metal grate and pull this person out of that pit. I was amazed and asked the Lord, "Lord, who did I just pray out of that pit?" His answer shocked me.

"You," He said. *Me*, I thought. *How did I get in there?* But I was so grateful to get out of there. I couldn't figure out how I got in there, but I couldn't wait to share this with my sister and Theresa. (Vision on the cover was painted by my friend and artist Pepsi Freund.) After all, I was a born-again, Holy-Spirit-filled Christian, so there had to be a huge mistake made here. So, I rushed back and called Theresa to tell her about the vision, and she said if God gave the vision, He would give the interpretation to it, so she prayed for me. Then we talked about our families, and I happened to mention that I was offended by how much my daughter adored my father more than me.

Theresa immediately stopped me. "That offense is a sin." I replied, "Well, wouldn't you be offended?" She then said I needed to repent for the sin of offense, and I did. She was very serious about it. I had no idea that a simple prayer of repentance would begin to open the door for the answers I so desperately needed. After reading several books on offense and hearing hundreds of tapes on forgiveness and other teachings, I would think, *Wouldn't this be a great book or tape for sister so and so?* They were the very people who offended me. Repentance is the key to the kingdom of heaven opening in your life. The church as a whole recites the general "Forgive Me, Lord" prayer for unforgiveness like a ritual. Then bring up sister so and so, who took ten dollars from your piggy bank and never paid you back, and the old resentment starts rising up to the surface, just like it happened yesterday.

About two weeks later, the Lord gave me a dream. In this dream, I was standing inside my former house in Illinois, where I was raised, and saw two demon spirits in the house. One looked like the wrestler Hulk Hogan with ratty hair and had a huge thick metal chain around its neck. The spirit walked into the living room saying, "What can I steal? What can I take?" The other spirit was in a bedroom with a brother of mine and said, "I love to gamble." Then I noticed that the front door was unlocked, and I ran to another room looking for my dad for help, and the back door was unlocked as well. The message was very clear. The Lord was showing me that there were spirits operating from my past that were stealing from me because I had "opened the doors" to them. The one like Hulk Hogan was the spirit of offense. Later, I discovered the one that loved to gamble was a spirit of deception. Now I knew that the problem was caused by these spirits, so I thanked the Lord for revealing this to me, and I repented and closed all the doors to those spirits, and yes, I called Theresa to tell her.

A few weeks later, during morning Bible reading, I opened to Matthew 18:7-9, where Jesus said:

> *Woe to the world because of offenses! For offenses must come, but woe to that man by whom the offense comes! If your hand or foot causes you to sin, cut it off and cast it from you. It is better for you to enter into life lame or maimed, rather than having two hands or two feet, to be cast into the everlasting fire. And if your eye causes you to sin, pluck it out and cast it from you. It is better for you to enter into life with one eye, rather than having two eyes, to be cast into hell fire.*

I was so amazed at this scripture I said, "Lord, You are so graphic here. Pluck out an eye, cut off a foot and hand? What do You mean by this?" Jesus was graphic here to prove a point. He is saying that whatever pain it may cause you or however much it hurts, cut off the offense from being received in your heart. Don't allow an offense.

You are the gatekeeper of your heart!

"Keep your heart with all diligence, for out of it spring the issues of life" (Proverbs 4:23). I went to work that same day, and Satan had a trap all set up for me at work to steal that word out of my heart. A girl in the office accused me of trying to get her in trouble after I asked our boss if I could help her relieve a heavy workload with a helping hand. He said, "No, thanks." But apparently, he told her about it, and she was mad! She approached me red in the face and screamed at me for saying anything to the boss about her. As I spoke the truth to her, the rage began to diminish some. Although she hadn't apologized to me, I remember this glorious peace that came all over me, not knowing that it came because of the scripture I had read that morning.

Psalm 119:165 says, *"Great peace have those who love Your law and nothing causes them to stumble."* Then the tapes started playing in my head, "Did you hear that? Just quit this stupid job! They don't pay you enough for this, Diane!" This was the spirit of offense speaking to me to get me to agree with it. Just then, out of my innermost being, these words came out of my mouth, "I choose not to be offended." I questioned this three times. The tapes that were playing in my head stopped immediately. I asked the Lord, "You mean I can choose not to allow an offense in my heart? I can choose to obey Your word and cut off the offense? Well, I choose Your word, Lord!" In total awe over this new peace, I called Theresa to tell her what happened. The Lord gave me a supernatural grace to stay in that job. Within two weeks, the person who came against me was fired for stealing from the company. I couldn't believe it. The woe came to her, the offender, and not me. Promoted to another job, which paid three times what I was making, I experienced a culture shock. They gave me days off and bonuses. I was blessed. Within two months, though, the offense attacks started again. The word would be tested. In Mark 4:3-9, 13-20, Jesus teaches a parable about the sower sowing seeds, and they get devoured, scorched, withered, and choked before being able to produce. Then He refers to seed as the word, and the enemy comes to steal it before it takes root. The enemy's greatest fear is that you would allow the word of God to produce in your life because when the truth is revealed, it not only blesses you, but it will be spirit and life given to others. Even after the promotion, a manager tested me, then another co-worker; then, another manager tried stealing funds from me that I earned.

I choose to not be offended; I choose to not be offended; I choose to not be offended!

I now know why Jesus said in Matthew 18:22 seventy times seven, you must forgive them. I was living this scripture. Through His grace and strength, I overcame the enemy of offense and chose to bless those who cursed me. Hearing them cursing me and accusing me was a very painful experience, but I also knew that the word of God would work, so I held my ground. Theresa had to agree with me many times in prayer. I spoke the truth to each one of them. The act of speaking the truth to the offender was so hard for me, but when it is done in a spirit of love, the Holy Spirit makes it easy. I knew that Satan would torment me again with all the accusations unless I exposed his plan. This is where so many miss it.

They go home quietly with arrows in their hearts, full of wounds and rejection. It was especially difficult when the offense came through an authority figure. Obedience to expose this darkness and get to the truth of a matter is more important than the sacrifice to approach someone. Many times, where I thought someone had said something about me, and they didn't, I just heard them wrong.

Satan tries to twist and pervert words all the time, so you hear it as an offense. Every time I spoke the truth, I received a new blessing from the Lord and a greater respect and a closer bonding with those Satan was attempting to sever from my life. Once again, everyone who came against me left the company within three months, and I remained with that company for two years. Praise the Lord! I left on good terms and went to work for the greatest Christian boss who paid me to pray! I would definitely say that was a divine turnaround. Had I held onto those offenses and bitterness, I know the pit of hell was waiting for me. When we hold unforgiveness, we are put in a debtor's prison and turned over to the tormentor. Jesus said it in Matthew 18:21-35 in the parable of the unforgiving servant, where a servant was forgiven a tremendous debt he could not repay. The master had compassion and forgave him, and he turned around and threw another servant that owed him some money into jail until he repaid the debt. The master was angry over the wicked servant's behavior, and he was delivered to torturers until he should pay back all the debt due him. In verse 35, Jesus says, *"So My heavenly Father also will do to you if each of you, from his heart, does not forgive his brother his trespasses."*

The pain it takes to say no to offense is nowhere compared to the tortures of hell's fire. But thanks to the almighty God, when I cried out to be free, He lifted the grate and let me go from the enemy's grips, and he can no longer have any hold on my life, nor yours. Psalm 34:17 says, *"The righteous cry out and the Lord hears, and delivers them out of all their troubles."*

I will never allow another offense to root in my heart. As Paul the Apostle stood up to his accusers in Acts 24:16, where he answers them, *"...I myself always strive to have a conscience without offense toward God and men,"* we must do the same!

If the spirit of offense has taken you captive, and you want to be free, obey the word and pray this prayer right now: "Father, in the name of Jesus, I repent for allowing a spirit of offense to enter my life. I am sorry for every offense that I have taken and for every offense that I have caused in others. I release and forgive every person who has offended me. Father, please forgive me and wash me in the precious blood of Jesus from this sin. I choose to never allow another offense to root into my heart. I choose to bless and not curse the ones who have offended me. Holy Spirit, please show me every offense I have taken and caused, and I will quickly repent. I dedicate my life to You, Lord Jesus. Come into my heart and fill my life with Your precious Holy Spirit. I love You and will obey and serve You all the days of my life. Thank You, Lord. Amen."

In Matthew 6:14-15, Jesus says, *"For if you forgive men their trespasses, your heavenly Father will also forgive you.*

But if you do not forgive men their trespasses, neither will your Father forgive your trespasses."

Please, allow me to pray for you:

"Father, in the name of Jesus Christ of Nazareth, I pray for this precious child of Yours, who You so love. Father, the enemy has bound them by the spirits of deception and offense, and now, because of repentance, I take the authority that You have given me as a believer, and I bind those spirits in Jesus' name from any further work and command them to go to the dry places and loose them right now! I declare and decree they have no more authority in their lives and must lose or release every hold on their minds. I command all the voices of offense to be stopped right now and smash spiritually every tape that has played in their mind. I declare freedom, liberty, and restoration of seven times for all that was stolen in Jesus' mighty name. Father, fill them up to overflow with Your love and peace, and I seal Your work with the blood of Jesus from head to toes over their life, ministry, and destiny. I ask that the arrows of the offenses be removed from their hearts now. I pray for the healing of those wounds. Lord, pour out the poison and pour in the new wine and oil and restore them to a greater place in You. Give them Your great discernment to recognize the offense coming against them so they can put a spiritual guard over their heart. Let them have the grace and strength to resist the enemy and cause him to flee from them. May they never forget how powerful Your word is in their lives.

"Draw them closer to You, Lord, every day. May they be free from offense till the day of Christ!

"Amen and amen."

"Of all acts of man repentance is the most divine. The greatest of all faults is to be conscious of none."

Thomas Carlyle

CHAPTER 4

I've Repented, Now What?

You have taken a powerful step in your new freedom, but remember that you may be challenged to see if this truth is really the truth. If Jesus said the enemy would try to come and steal this word, then you can rest assured that future offenses may be sent your way. But now you are armed and dangerous to the dark kingdom. Next, you must be a gatekeeper to your heart, only allowing truth to remain. Keep every door to the enemy shut tightly. Should there be any negative thoughts that come against your mind toward someone, picture yourself placing those deadly words in a box, sealing it, and laying at the foot of the cross. Then, leave it there. Any time it tries to resurrect, send it back to the cross, and the enemy will give up. He has no power over you except what you allow him to have.

Believe the work of the cross was finished and Satan's power has no more hold over you or any of your loved ones. I have asked the Holy Spirit to expose every offense that has not been resolved and hinders your relationship with Him and others; when He does, just quickly repent, release, and forgive that person, and if there is anything more needed, the Lord will lay it on your heart. Always obey; freedom is just ahead. He may have you phone the person, write them a letter, or see them in person to resolve the offense. Obviously, if the person is deceased, there is nothing more you can do except repent and allow the Holy Spirit to represent them. He is the greatest intercessor (go-between), and He can talk to that person for you. This is vital for women who have been raped, molested, or had abortions.

The enemy loves to use these things to torment the minds of believers, especially when the person you offended is dead. The accuser of the brethren will try to bring condemnation to you to make you unqualified as a believer. Do not agree with the adversary; repent and watch the Lord set you free. Jesus came to destroy the works of the enemy. Romans 8:26 says, *"Likewise the Spirit also helps in our weaknesses. For we do not know what we should pray for as we ought, but the Spirit Himself makes intercession for us with groanings which cannot be uttered."*

Holy Spirit will bring closure and refreshing to you as you open your heart to Him. He already knows everything, but we are to confess our sins in order to be released. The hardest person to forgive is usually yourself, but you must forgive everyone, or your Father in heaven won't forgive you. In the "Our Father" model prayer in Matthew 6:12, Jesus said, *"And forgive us our debts, as [in the same manner as] we forgive our debtors."* When you repent and the Lord cleanses you and His precious love and mercy say you are forgiven, then you'll have a reunion to look forward to, and the sins of the past are under the blood of Jesus, never to be remembered again. It is your responsibility to be obedient to His word; it is His to bring the healing and restoration that is needed.

There are two recorded offenses in the Bible: 1 Samuel 25:2-32, where David is running from King Saul, who wants to kill him. David becomes very hungry, asking for food. So, he sends a messenger asking for food from a wealthy man named Nabal, who lives close by. Nabal says "No way" to the messenger, and when his report is given to David, he becomes offended. David actually stays awake all night plotting how to kill Nabal for neglecting him in his hour of need. David had protected Nabal from harm coming his way the entire time he was in Carmel and felt Nabal owed him a great favor.

Thank heaven Abigail (Nabal's wife) had intercepted the offense and brought food to David. Nabal died for his greed, but Abigail was spared and blessed tremendously. The second example is found in Matthew 11:1-6, where John the Baptist is thrown into prison for preaching truth to Herod. John had no fear of man and was very obedient to his call. He was in the Jordan River when the heavens opened and the Father announced Jesus as His beloved Son in whom He was well pleased. Surprisingly, now he's questioning if Jesus is the one or if we should look for another? Sounds like doubt came in after the offense.

Jesus replied, "Go and tell John the things which you hear and see: The blind see and the lame walk; the lepers are cleansed, and the deaf hear; the dead are raised up, and the poor have the gospel preached to them. And blessed is he who is not offended because of Me." James 3:2 says, "For we all stumble in many things. If anyone does not stumble in word, he is a perfect man, able also to bridle the whole body." The word "perfect" here means "mature, whole, and complete." The Lord wants to restore, heal and deliver us in every area of our lives. He will then strip the things that hold us back from drawing closer to Him. Each time He does, simply surrender to Him and repent. I pray for you as the Apostle Paul prayed:

> ...that your love may abound still more and more in knowledge and all discernment, that you may approve the things that are excellent, that you may be sincere and without offense till the day of Christ, being filled with fruits of righteousness which are by Jesus Christ, to the glory and praise of God.
>
> Philippians 1:9-11

The blessing of the Lord is always released upon our obedience to His word.

"God's ways, God's results, every time!"

Diane Bernardin

CHAPTER 5

The Spirit-Led Walk

For many years I've searched for answers to living a successful Spirit-led life, where the tangible evidence of His almighty presence would be seen upon my life. Where others would tell me, "I don't know what it is you have gotten a hold of, but I know I need what you've got!" I have literally had women angry with me over the joy they see in me. One woman actually screamed, "*Stop laughing!*" You will definitely encounter some strange reactions from some individuals who do not understand the joy that you can truly have in Christ. Have you grown tired of trying to lead your own life? You seem to take one step forward and several backward? I had such a desperate longing to serve the Lord wholeheartedly and walk in His pathway and no longer my own.

A Spirit-led walk is possible for every believer who is willing and desires to have all that God desires rather than the self-controlled life that many believers walk in. One of the greatest truths I learned is that this walk is all about Him. It is truly a selfless life. The greatest desire of your heart should be spiritual hunger. Knowing there is so much more that the Lord desires to reveal to us, we can truly seek after Him and will find Him if we seek with all of our heart. At times, He will interrupt your quiet world to reveal His glorious will and desire toward another.

It may be just a "Jesus loves you" to someone having an awful day. Jesus prayed to His Father to send the Holy Spirit to you, so you would not have to walk alone and that you would discover the glorious, abundant life that He has purchased and desires for you to have as He guides your every step. You can obtain a place of rest where you hear the spirit of God speak to you as you listen to Him and yield to Him. In order to obtain such a life, we must take a journey together. This will be a journey where you will meet the Father, Son, and Holy Spirit and not just know about them, but discover that you can know them. Before we begin, let's pray, "Heavenly Father, we come before You, hungering and thirsting for more revelation, wisdom, and understanding of what the Spirit-led walk is, and Father, please allow our ears to hear, our eyes to see, and our hearts to receive all You have to teach us as we search out Your truth. Anoint our eyes with eye salve and let every seed of Your word be richly planted in us. May we know You and the power of Your resurrection. I pray in Jesus' mighty and glorious name, amen."

"Those blessings are sweetest that are won with prayers and won with thanks."

Thomas Goodwin

CHAPTER 6

In Everything Give Thanks

"In everything give thanks; for this is the will of God in Christ Jesus for you" (1 Thessalonians 5:18). I know that it may seem ridiculous to some of you to give thanks to the Lord for everything in this life, whether good or bad, but this is the will of God. Although it doesn't make sense to the carnal mind, there is something in heaven that is released when we give thanks to the Lord. This truth will transform your life as you apply it in everything. There is another side to every circumstance that we encounter in this life. You may be going through one of the hardest battles of your life, but the truth is, you are going through to the other side of it. I am so grateful the Lord taught me the power of thanksgiving.

I have watched numerous circumstances turn from disaster to victory as the stand to give thanks is made. *"But thanks be to God, who gives us the victory through our Lord Jesus Christ"* (1 Corinthians 15:57). Throughout the Bible, many miracles occurred through the giving of thanks to the Lord for His mercy, healing, and provision. Look at the miracle of the feeding of the five thousand:

> *After these things Jesus went over the Sea of Galilee, which is the Sea of Tiberias. Then a great multitude followed Him, because they saw His signs which He performed on those who were diseased. And Jesus went up on the mountain, and there He sat with His disciples. Now the Passover, a feast of the Jews, was near. Then Jesus lifted up His eyes, and seeing a great multitude coming toward Him, He said to Philip, "Where shall we buy bread that these may eat?" But this He said to test him, for He Himself knew what He would do.*
> *Philip answered Him, "Two hundred denarii worth of bread is not sufficient for them, that every one of them may have a little." One of His disciples, Andrew, Simon Peter's brother, said to him, "There is a lad here who has five barley loaves and two small fish, but what are they among so many?" Then Jesus said, "Make the people sit down." Now there was much grass in the place. So the men sat down, in number about five thousand. And Jesus took the loaves, and when He had given thanks, He distributed them to the disciples, and the disciples to those sitting down; and likewise of the fish, as*

*much as they wanted. So when they were filled,
He said to His disciples, "Gather up the fragments
that remain, so that nothing is lost." Therefore they
gathered them up, and filled twelve baskets with the
fragments of the five barley loaves which were left
over by those who had eaten.*

John 6:1-13

I am thankful to God daily for salvation, deliverance, healing, and most of all, His grace over my life. How can we not be thankful when He gave us so much, and all we need to do is receive these wonderful promises. I remember a time when my husband Michel and I were traveling across the Idaho desert in our Honda Accord, and the radiator kept overheating on us. There was a great stretch of roadway that had a creek alongside it, and anytime we overheated, Michel would pull off the road and fill the water bottles full and cool the car down. I was so thankful to the Lord for the provision of that creek to assist us. Well, we had enough water to get us part of the way to the next town, which was over fifteen miles, and we had nothing but sand and heat on either side of us. Michel used every ounce of water up to keep the vehicle going, but he ran out of water. Up went the temperature gauge, and he said, "Diane, unless the Lord intervenes, we are at the end of the trail."

We kept thanking the Lord and prayed in the Spirit. We came to a curve in the road, and just as the car began to smoke again, we looked to see something so amazing on the other side of the curve, a spring of water that filled up the middle of the road. We looked at each other amazed. Our Lord had provided an oasis in the desert, literally! There was nothing but sand everywhere, and here out, in the middle of nowhere, there is water. Michel was concerned that he wouldn't be able to cross over the water with the car, as he wasn't sure how deep it was.

All of a sudden, these two men pull up to the road in a vehicle similar to an ATV. Michel asked them if it was safe to cross, and they said yes and drove through as if to demonstrate for us. He asked them how far to the next town, and they said twelve miles. So he filled the bottles up again with water. I truly believe those two men were angels. The water was the exact amount needed to get us to the next town. We had our camera with us and took pictures of that miracle oasis in the desert. Whatever attack you may encounter in this life, if you will give the Lord the thanks and praise through it, He will begin to turn things around in His timing, not ours.

Michel at the oasis the Lord created.
Michel calls Him Jehovah nick of time!

When I think of the miracle of Lazarus:

> *Now a certain man was sick, named Lazarus, of*
> *Bethany, the town of Mary and her sister Martha.*
> *(It was that Mary who anointed the Lord with fra-*
> *grant oil, and wiped his feet with her hair, whose*
> *brother Lazarus was sick.) Therefore His sisters*
> *sent to him, saying, "Lord, behold, he whom you*
> *love is sick." When Jesus heard that, He said, "This*
> *sickness is not unto death, but for the glory of God,*
> *that the Son of God may be glorified through it."*

Now Jesus loved Martha, and her sister, and Lazarus. When He had heard that he was sick, He stayed two more days in the place where he was. Then after this He said to the disciples, "Let us go to Judea again." The disciples said to him, "Rabbi, lately the Jews sought to stone You; and are You going there again? "Jesus answered, "Are there not twelve hours in the day? If anyone walks in the day, he does not stumble, because he sees the light of this world. But if one walks in the night, he stumbles, because the light is not in him." These things He said: and after that He said to them, "Our friend Lazarus sleeps; but I go, that I may wake him up." Then His disciples said, "Lord, if he sleeps, he will get well." However, Jesus spoke of his death: but they thought that he was speaking about taking rest in sleep. Then Jesus said to them plainly, "Lazarus is dead. And I am glad for your sakes that I was not there, that you may believe. Nevertheless let us go to him."

Then said Thomas, which is called the Twin, said to his fellow disciples, "Let us also go, that we may die with him." So when Jesus came, He found that he had already been in the grave four days. Now Bethany was near Jerusalem, about two miles away. And many of the Jews had joined the women around Martha and Mary, to comfort them concerning their brother. Then Martha, as soon as she heard that Je-

sus was coming, went and met him: but Mary was sitting in the house. Now Martha said to Jesus, "Lord, if you had been here, my brother would not have died. But even now I know, that whatever You ask of God, God will give You."

Jesus said to her, "Your brother will rise again." Martha said to Him, "I know that he will rise again in the resurrection at the last day.' "Jesus said to her, "I am the resurrection, and the life: he who believes in Me, though he may die, he shall live. And whosoever lives and believes in Me shall never die. Do you believe this?" She said to him, "Yes, Lord: I believe that you are the Christ, the Son of God, who is to come into the world." And when she had said these things, she went her way, and secretly called Mary her sister, saying, "The Teacher has come and is calling for you." As soon as she heard that, she arose quickly, and came to Him. Now Jesus had not yet come into the town, but was in the place where Martha met him.

Then the Jews who were with her in the house, and comforting her, when they saw that Mary rose up quickly and went out, followed her, saying, "She is going to the tomb to weep there." Then when Mary came where Jesus was, and saw him, she fell down at his feet, saying to him, "Lord, if you had been here, my brother would not have died." Therefore, when Jesus saw her weeping, and the Jews who came with her weeping, He groaned in the spirit, and was troubled. And said, "Where have you laid him?" They said to him, "Lord, come and see." Jesus wept. Then the Jews said, "See how He loved him!" And some of them said, "Could not this man, who opened the eyes of the blind, also have kept this man from dying?" Then Jesus, again groaning in Himself, came to the tomb. It was a cave, and a stone lay against it. Jesus said, "Take away the stone." Martha, the sister of him who was dead, said to him, "Lord, by this time there is a stench, for he has been dead four days." Jesus said to her, "Did I not say to you that, if you would believe, you would see the glory of God?" Then they took away the stone from the place where the dead man was lying. And Jesus lifted up his eyes, and said, "Father, I thank You that You have heard me. And I know that You always hear Me, but because of the people who are standing by I said this, that they may believe that You sent Me." Now when He had said these things, He cried with a loud voice, "Lazarus, come forth!" And he who had died came out, bound hand and foot with grave clothes, and his face was wrapped with a cloth. Jesus said to them, "Loose him, and let him go."

John 11:1-44

Jesus is our primary example regarding giving thanks, whether in His prayers to His Father or before a meal; Jesus always gave Him thanks, praise, and glory. As we follow His direction and won't doubt, we will see our miracle.

> *Rejoice in the Lord always. Again I will say rejoice! Let your gentleness be known to all men. The Lord is at hand. Be anxious for nothing, but in everything by prayer and supplication, with thanksgiving, let your requests be made known to God; and the peace of God, which surpasses all understanding, will guard your hearts and minds through Christ Jesus.*
>
> Philippians 4:4-7

This is the miracle of peace that will protect you in the center of any storm you are facing. In regards to cheerful giving, there is a special blessing with giving thanks:

> *Now may He who supplies seed to the sower, and bread for food, supply and multiply the seed you have sown and increase the fruits of your righteousness, while you are enriched in everything for all liberality, which causes thanksgiving through us to God. For the administration of this service not only supplies the needs of the saints, but also is abound-*

*ing through many thanksgivings to God, while,
through the proof of this ministry, they glorify God
for the obedience of your confession to the gospel of
Christ, and for your liberal sharing with them and
all men, and by their prayer for you, who long for
you because of the exceeding grace of God in you.*

2 Corinthians 9:10-14

People will take notice when you walk in God's grace, and some will long to have the same blessing upon their life. I have seen the Lord turn many things around supernaturally as I give Him the honor with a thankful heart ahead of His provision, whether I see the answer right away or not. He releases His supernatural peace in my heart that guards it against care and anxiety. He deserves the honor so richly due Him. Remember He is our king, and a king deserves the highest honor of all! He is the King of kings and Lord of lords.

Here is the blessing of healing through thanksgiving:

*Now it happened as He went to Jerusalem that He
passed through the midst of Samaria and Galilee.
Then as He entered a certain village, there met Him
ten men who were lepers, who stood afar off. And
they lifted up their voices, and said, "Jesus, Master, have mercy on us!" So when He saw them, He
said to them, "Go, show yourselves to the priests."*

And so it was that as they went, they were cleansed. And one of them, when he saw that he was healed, returned, and with a loud voice glorified God, and fell down on his face at His feet, giving him thanks. And he was a Samaritan. So Jesus answered and said, "Were there not ten cleansed? But where are the nine? Were there not any found who returned to give glory to God except this foreigner?" And He said to him, "Arise, go your way. Your faith has made you well."

Luke 17:11-19

Here are ten men desperately pleading to Jesus for healing from leprosy. Jesus instructs them to show themselves to the priests because, according to Leviticus law (Leviticus 13:2-3), the priests would pronounce the leper clean or unclean (to purge or purify). There is not enough information as to why the other nine would not give thanks. They may have been Jewish because Jesus refers to the Samaritan as a foreigner. Healing was the children's bread, so they probably were expecting their healing based on this truth. The Samaritan saw himself healed, and by faith, he came to offer thanks ahead of the time that the priest declared him clean. Jesus said his faith made him well (saved, protected, and delivered). In an alternate translation, the Samaritan received salvation as well as his physical healing because of thanksgiving.

Let's pray: "Father, I ask in Jesus' name that You would grant me a thankful heart for everything and in everything that I am to encounter here in this life, whether it is good or not. You are more than able to turn every situation around by Your mighty power. I thank You for all You have done and, most of all, who You are in my life. I make the declaration that You are Lord over every area of my life, and You are the Lord of divine turnaround. And Lord, I want to thank You for hearing me when I pray for my needs as well as others', and please forgive me for the times I have not been thankful, for I have so much to be thankful for, healing, salvation, and glorious deliverance. All in the mighty name of Jesus, the name above every name, amen."

"It's not what you did, but what you could have done if you allowed the Lord to work His will in your life."

A.W. Tozer

CHAPTER 7

You Must Know God to Trust God

"Trust in the Lord with all your heart and lean not to your own understanding; in all your ways acknowledge Him, and He shall direct your paths" (Proverbs 3:5-6). This was the scripture given to me by the Lord when I prayed to Him regarding what I was called to do for Him with my life. In order to trust the Lord, you must know Him. There is a big difference between knowing about God and knowing God. The number one way to know Him is to spend time with Him in His Word. The Word of God will reveal the Father, Son, and Holy Spirit (the triune God) to us. Another way to know Him is through prayer (simply communicating with Him from your heart to His). Prayer is not a formula.

Jesus taught His disciples to pray to the Father, glorifying His name, His kingdom, and His will. He will respond as a loving Father to your heart, crying out for His help, which moves Him deeply, and He will listen.

Look at His promise, *"The righteous cry out, and the Lord hears, and delivers them out of all of their troubles"* (Psalm 34:17). I am so grateful the Lord hears me when I pray, and He delivers me because He loves me and has shown me that He is love.

The Triune God

"Hear, O Israel: The Lord our God, the Lord is one! You shall love the Lord your God with all your heart, with all your soul, and with all your strength" (Deuteronomy 6:4-5). There are not three different Gods. *"I am the Lord, and there is no other; There is no God besides Me"* (Isaiah 45:5). *"... there is no other God but one"* (1 Corinthians 8:4). As you can clearly see, there is only one God. But He has three different forms. God is a spirit. The Word tells us God, our Father, abides in Heaven. *"Our Father in heaven, hallowed be Your name"* (Matthew 6:9).

Our heavenly Father lives in heaven, but when we receive Jesus Christ as our Lord and have the Holy Spirit living inside of our spiritual heart, the Word says the fullness of the Godhead dwells in us bodily. *"There is one body and one Spirit, just as you were called in one hope of your calling; one Lord, one faith, one baptism; one God and Father of all, who is above all, and through all, and in you all"* (Ephesians 4:4-6). You can see the oneness again as Jesus said, *"I and My Father are one"* (John 10:30) and *"He who has seen Me has seen the Father; so how can you say, 'Show us* the Father'?" (John 14:9) and *"And he who sees Me sees Him who sent Me"* (John 12:45). *"Now when He was asked by the Pharisees when the kingdom of God would come, He answered them and said, 'The kingdom of God does not come with observation; nor will they say, "See Here!" or "See there!" For indeed, the kingdom of God is within you'"* (Luke 17:20-21). Even the significance of the kingdom of God living within us was prophesied by Jesus regarding the baptism of the Holy Spirit coming to live in us as living temples and will transform us into His image.

> *No one has seen God at any time. If we love one another, God abides in us, and His love has been perfected in us. By this we know that we abide in Him and He in us, because He has given us of His Spirit. And we have seen and testify that the Father has sent the Son as Savior of the world. Whoever confesses that Jesus is the Son of God, God abides in him, and he in God. And we have known and believed the love that God has for us. God is love, and he who abides in love abides in God, and God in him.*
>
> 1 John 4:12-17

Father God sent His Son and His Holy Spirit to the earth to carry out His divine will and plan for the redemption of sinful mankind. From the beginning, He intended to have a different plan for us. *"Then God said, 'Let Us make man in Our image, according to Our likeness; let them have dominion over the fish of the sea, over the birds of the air, and over the cattle, over all the earth, and over every creeping thing that creeps on the earth'"* (Genesis 1:26). We were created to take dominion and rule over all the earth as a spirit, created in the image of God, and dwell in an earthly body here on the earth.

When we die, our spirit man will leave our body and enter the presence of the Lord in heaven, but our earthly body will remain here on earth. "We are confident, I say, yes well pleased rather to be absent from the body and to be present with the Lord" (2 Corinthians 5:8). We then begin to see the love God has for man, to restore the original relationship that was lost through Adam's sin. In order to accomplish this, there had to be a price paid for the sin of mankind as *"...the wages of sin is death..."* (Romans 6:23), and without the shedding of blood, there was no remission for sin. The old covenant law required that blood was shed from calves and goats to atone for sin until Jesus willingly came to die in our place. *"For God so loved the world that He gave His only begotten Son, that whoever believes in Him should not perish but have everlasting life"* (John 3:16).

The sinless Lamb of God, Jesus, comes to our earth as a fleshly man, laying aside all deity, to pay the price for our sin as a willing, spotless sacrifice.

In the beginning was the Word, and the Word was with God, and the Word was God. He was in the beginning with God. All things were made through Him, and without Him nothing was made that was made. And the Word became flesh and dwelt among us, and we beheld His glory, the glory as of the only begotten of the Father, full of grace and truth.

John 1:1-3,14

John the Baptist was present to witness heaven's special announcement:

When He had been baptized, Jesus came up immediately from the water; and behold, the heavens were opened to Him, and He saw the Spirit of God descending like a dove, and alighting upon Him. And suddenly a voice came from heaven, saying, "This is My beloved Son, in whom I am well pleased."

Matthew 3:16-17

Here we see the Trinity in full manifestation and operating together. When Jesus taught His disciples, He released this commission, *"Go therefore and make disciples of all the nations, baptizing them in the name of the Father and of the Son and of the Holy Spirit, teaching them to observe all things that I have commanded you; and lo; I am with you always, even to the end of the age. Amen"* (Matthew 28:19-20). There has been much controversy over whose name we should baptize in. The scripture is very clear here. It came from the mouth of Jesus Himself.

He also refers to two baptisms, one with water and one with the Holy Spirit (fire). In John chapter 3, He tells the story of being born again of the water and the spirit in order to enter the kingdom of God. *"Now if anyone does not have the Spirit of Christ, he is not His"* (Romans 8:9). *"Joseph, son of David, do not be afraid to take to you Mary your wife; for that which is conceived in her is of the Holy Spirit"* (Matthew 1:20). *"And the angel answered and said to her [Mary], 'The Holy Spirit will come upon you, and the power of the Highest will overshadow you; therefore, also, that Holy One who is to be born will be called the Son of God'"* (Luke 1:35).

Jesus speaking to His disciples:

> *And I will pray the Father, and He will give you another Helper, that He may abide with you forever; the Spirit of truth, whom the world cannot receive, because it neither sees Him nor knows Him; but you know Him, for He dwells with you and will be in you. I will not leave you orphans; I will come to you...If anyone loves Me, he will keep my word; and My Father will love him, and We will come to him and make Our home with him...But the Helper,*

the Holy Spirit, whom the Father will send in My name, He will teach you all things, and bring to your remembrance all things that I said to you.

John 14:16-18, 23, 26

"For in Him [Christ] dwells all the fullness of the Godhead bodily" (Colossians 2:9). "To them God willed to make known what are the riches of the glory of this mystery among the Gentiles: which is Christ in you, the hope of glory" (Colossians 1:27). We can see the revelation of the word "fullness" above in Paul's prayer:

For this reason I bow my knees to the Father of our Lord Jesus Christ, from whom the whole family in heaven and earth is named, that He would grant you, according to the riches of His glory, to be strengthened with might through His Spirit in the inner man, that Christ may dwell in your hearts through faith; that you being rooted and grounded in love, may be able to comprehend with all the saints what is the width and length and depth and height, to know the love of Christ which passes knowledge; that you may be filled with all the fullness of God. Now to Him who is able to do exceedingly abundantly above all that we ask or think, according to the power that works in us.

Ephesians 3:14-20

When we have the person of the Holy Spirit living inside of us, we have the Father, Son, and Holy Spirit as they are all one and the same God. *"For the kingdom of God is not eating and drinking, but righteousness, and peace and joy in the Holy Spirit"* (Romans 14:17). *"Do you not know that you are the temple of God and that the Spirit of God dwells in you?"* (1 Corinthians 3:16)

I recall an encounter I had shortly after being baptized in the Holy Spirit at my sister's church. I was at home lying in bed, and the Lord gave me an open vision where I saw a candlelit room that was very dark. There were candles set on a table at the left of this room. I saw myself standing in the room, and all of a sudden, the Holy Spirit walked out of me. I saw the brightest light radiate from Him. The whole room was illuminated from His presence. He wore a glistening white robe with a golden belt and had snow-white hair about shoulder length. He held a glowing sword in His right hand. He walked over to a man who was kneeling, and his head was down. I watched Him take the sword and place it upon his shoulder.

Right afterward, He turned around and looked at me. His eyes were so bright, like two balls of the sun. He extended His arms out and began to walk back toward me and then walked into me, and the room was dark again. I woke up realizing that He lived inside of me. I told my sister, Sharon, about it, and she showed me in the book of Revelation 1:12-16 where John saw Christ in His glory. I was so blessed to have this encounter with Him. It created such a hunger to know all about Him. I also knew I could call upon Him at any time, and He would hear me. Now, you can see clearly the reality of the triune God, Father, Son, and Holy Spirit. You can see they are all one with each other yet have the ability to be in various places at the same time; they are omnipresent. Now, let's discover the character of God.

"The Lord is a man of war: the Lord is his name" (Exodus 15:3). God is a protector! *"The Lord is longsuffering, and abundant in mercy, forgiving iniquity and transgression; but He by no means clears the guilty, visiting the iniquity of the fathers on the children to the third and fourth generation"* (Numbers 14:18).

"The Lord is in His holy temple, the Lord's throne is in heaven; His eyes behold, His eyelids test the sons of men" (Psalm 11:4). *"The secret of the Lord is with those that fear Him, and He will show them His covenant"* (Psalm 25:14). As we fear (highly reverence) the Lord, He will begin to confirm the reality of His holiness and the validity of His covenant promises to us in His Word. He will manifest Himself to us in various ways; dreams, visions, audible voices, angelic visitations, and His word laborers. *"The voice of the Lord is over the waters; the God of glory thunders; the Lord is over many waters. The voice of the Lord is powerful; the voice of the Lord is full of majesty"* (Psalm 29:3-4).

He will train us to hear His voice clearly, through the inner witness (still small voice) inside. There are times He will speak audible, either directly to us or through another believer. *"The Lord is my shepherd; I shall not want"* (Psalm 23:1). He is our great provider who already knows all we have a need of before we even ask Him. *"Behold, the eye of the Lord is on those that fear Him, on those who hope in His mercy"* (Psalm 33:18). He watches over our ways as we trust in His leading and guiding of our lives. This is a powerful truth, knowing that our Lord watches over all that we do. *"O taste and see that the Lord is good; blessed is the man who trusts in Him!"* (Psalm 34:8) There is a blessing released over the one who first focuses on His beautiful face through worship, then trusts (relies totally upon) the Lord.

"The face of the Lord is against those who do evil, to cut off the remembrance of them from the earth...The Lord is near to those who have a broken heart, and saves such as have a contrite spirit" (Psalm 34:16, 18). The Lord resists those who are full of pride because they have no need of His leading; they want to control their own lives and remain independent. Allowing the Lord to break the hardness of the heart and change us into His image, we then become completely dependent upon Him. *"The Lord reigns, He is clothed with majesty; the Lord is clothed, He has girded Himself with strength. Surely the world is established, so that it cannot be moved"* (Psalm 93:1). *"He has made His wonder-*

ful works to be remembered; the Lord is gracious and full of compassion" (Psalm 111:4). *"For the Lord is our Judge, the Lord is our lawgiver, the Lord is our King; He will save us"* (Isaiah 33:22) *"For the eyes of the Lord are on the righteous, and His ears are open to their prayers; but the face of the Lord is against those who do evil"* (1 Peter 3:12). *"The Lord is not slack concerning His promise, as some men count slackness, but is long suffering toward us, not willing that any should perish but that all should come to repentance"* (2 Peter 3:9).

You Can Trust Him

"He who dwells in the secret place of the Most High shall abide under the shadow of the Almighty. I will say of the Lord, 'He is my refuge and my fortress; my God, in Him I will trust'" (Psalm 91:1-3). The Lord will fight the battle for us against our enemy. He will protect us from harm. He will hide us in the secret place of His presence as we draw closer in prayer, feed on His Word, and seek His beautiful face.

He is a God who fulfills every one of His promises to us. *"Offer the sacrifices of righteousness, and put your trust in the Lord"* (Psalm 4:5). The definition found for "trust" is "to be confident or sure, be bold (confident, secure, sure), careless, put confidence, (make to) hope, (put, make to) trust, to flee for protection, figuratively to confide in: have hope, make refuge." *"The Lord is my rock and my fortress and my deliverer; My God, my strength, in whom I will trust; My shield and the horn of my salvation, my stronghold"* (Psalm 18:2). *"As for God, His way is perfect; the word of the Lord is proven; He is a shield to all who trust in Him"* (Psalm 18:30). *"Commit your way to the Lord, trust also in Him, and He shall bring it to pass"* (Psalm 37:5). *"And the Lord shall help them and deliver them; He shall deliver them from the wicked, and save them, because they trust in Him"* (Psalm 37:40).

> *The Lord gives voice before His army, For His camp is very great; For strong is the One who executes His word. For the day of the Lord is great and very terrible; Who can endure it? "Now, therefore," says the Lord, "turn to Me with all your heart, with fasting, with weeping, and with mourning." So, rend your heart, and not your garments; Return to the Lord your God, for He is gracious and merciful, slow to anger, and of great kindness; and He relents from doing harm.*
>
> *Who knows if He will return and relent, and leave a blessing behind Him; a grain offering and a drink offering for the Lord your God?*
>
> Joel 2:11-14

These scriptures clearly show the merciful and loving heart of our Lord. He is always looking for us to draw close to Him so He can show His powerful love to us, protect us, bless us, and heal us. I purposed to expose His heart to you through His word, not my opinion.

Let's pray: "Father, I thank You for revealing to me Your heart of love for me. I want to know more and more. Create in me a clean heart, Father. Renew a right spirit within me. I repent for allowing any idols into my heart and life. I give You permission, Holy Spirit, to cleanse me from all unrighteous thoughts and deeds done through this carnal flesh. I desire to know You and ask for encounters with You. Reveal yourself to me, Lord. I pray, in Jesus' mighty name I pray, amen."

"Do not go where the path may lead; go instead where there is no path and leave a trail."

Ralph Waldo Emerson

CHAPTER 8

His Word & Your Prayers

Jesus taught His disciples to pray. His "Model Prayer" says:

> *And when you pray, you shall not be like the hypo-crites. For they love to pray standing in the syna-gogues and on the corners of the streets, that they may be seen of men. Assuredly, I say to you, they have their reward. But you, when you pray, go into your room, and when you have shut your door, pray to your Father who is in the secret place; and your Father who sees in secret will reward you openly. And when you pray, do not use vain repetitions as the heathen do. For they think that they will be heard for their many words.*
>
> *Therefore do not be like them. For your Father knows the things you have need of before you ask Him. In this manner, therefore, pray: Our Father in heaven,*

Hallowed be your name. Your kingdom come. Your will be done on earth as it is in heaven. Give us this day our daily bread. And forgive us our debts, as we forgive our debtors. And do not lead us into temptation, but deliver us from the evil one. For yours is the kingdom and the power and the glory forever. Amen. For if you forgive men their trespasses, your heavenly Father will also forgive you. But if you do not forgive men their trespasses, neither will your Father forgive your trespasses.

Matthew 6:5-15

I will go into this prayer in detail in the next chapter, but this is a prayer that should be memorized and sown into your heart as divine wisdom from our Lord Jesus.

"So shall My word be that goes forth from My mouth; It shall not return to Me void, but shall accomplish what I please, And it shall prosper in the thing in which I sent it" (Isaiah 55:11). His word is forever settled here on earth as it is in heaven. It is powerful, and it will produce as we send it forth in prayer. *"For as the body without the spirit is dead, so faith without works is dead also"* (James 2:26). You see, when you meditate on the Word of God, it produces faith in your heart. The type of faith produced is whatever promise you choose to meditate on. The Scripture promise should be meditated on until it passes from your mind into your heart by the Holy Spirit, and He

will bring the Word back to your remembrance when you face certain tests or trials.

"But without faith it is impossible to please Him; for he who comes to God must believe that He is, and that He is a rewarder of those who diligently seek Him" (Hebrews 11:6). For faith to produce in our lives, we must stand firm in our confession of His powerful Word and don't ever give up on our stand. Faith is not according to your need as your need does not move God. Many believe that if God doesn't respond to our prayers for healing or deliverance, He doesn't hear us and that it must be His will for us to remain sick or tormented. The Lord will heal and deliver us, as it is one of His benefits.

"Bless the Lord O my soul and all that is within me bless His holy name. Bless the Lord O my soul and forget not all His benefits. Who forgives all your iniquities and heals all your diseases" (Psalm 103:1-3). This is a very clear picture of the will of our Lord toward our health and sin. He is a restorer and healer to those who believe in Him. It brings Him tremendous glory to manifest His kingdom in our lives. We receive a special blessing as we bless the Lord with all our souls! Amen.

"Heaven will be the perfection we've always longed for. All the things that made Earth unlovely and tragic will be absent in heaven."

Billy Graham

CHAPTER 9

Intercessory Prayer and True Repentance

There are actually several types of prayer the Lord teaches us about in the Scriptures. The first, of course, is the prayer of petition. Jesus gives clear instruction as to how to pray to the Father (Matthew 6:9-15). I want to hear from God, and I want to have answers to the prayers that I pray to Him. The most important thing I could ever advise when you pray is to speak from your heart to God. David said in Psalm 139:7-12 there was no place he could run to that He was not there with him. Be real before Him as He already knows everything you have need of and is more than willing to meet that need. He delights in the time you spend reading His Word and praying with Him, and as your heart is open before Him, be patient and willing to allow Him to speak into your heart His answer. Many of us pray a short prayer, and if there is no immediate response from God, we conclude our time with Him.

Prayer to the Lord should be a continual process, and we can relate to Him as a child relates to his father. The most exciting prayers I discovered are the prayers of true repentance and the prayer of intercession. The results I have received are amazing to me, and I pray they will encourage you to bring repentance where He leads you to and be faithful to pray when His burden comes upon you. Many years ago, I saw the movie Geronimo at the theater and was absolutely enraged for the poor Indians that were treated so horrifically by our government. I left that movie weeping, and a burden for the Indian nations came on me. I prayed silently, "Lord, should I ever come across an Indian brother or sister related to *Geronimo*, I would apologize to them for that awful cruelty displayed over greed and control." I prayed that the Lord would somehow make that up to them and bring restoration to them if they would ever receive it. About two years ago, as Michel and I were traveling across the country, we noticed a little shop in North Carolina where they sold Indian clothes, pottery, and similar items.

What caught our attention was "Geronimo" in the shop name. Something inside of me jumped, and so we decided to go in and look around. When we went to check out, there was a precious Indian man there, and

I felt led by the Spirit to mention Geronimo to him. He startled me by saying he was an actual descendant of Geronimo. Here is my chance, I thought. I asked him if I could stand in the gap and say how sorry I am as an American for the horrible way Geronimo was treated and asked him if he would please forgive me. He was shocked at first but replied, "Yes, I will." What a moment! What a privilege to be a part of that moment. Does God hear intercession? I am blessed to be a descendant of Aaron Burr Sr.'s lineage through my grandfather on my mother's side of the family. The exact link to him is unknown as the birth records were not recorded well during those years. Her father was a photographer, and there was a photograph passed down through the years of Abe Lincoln, which was a *carte de visite* or calling card. During my years of research online, I came across the exact picture connected to a family up north. I was so excited to find a similar picture, so I emailed the lady who had it, and she said she found it in the attic, and it belonged to her grandfather, who was a general in the picture. I asked her questions, but she didn't know anything about it either. I told her that it came through the Burr family, and I was a descendant, and she said, "Really?"

I said, "Yes." She said she was a descendant of Alexander Hamilton. I was amazed. I asked her if she knew if anyone in the Burr family ever asked for forgiveness for the murder of Alexander Hamilton, and she didn't think so. I felt the presence of the Lord as I asked her by email to please allow me to stand in the gap for the Burr family and say how sorry I was that the murder occurred and ask if they would forgive us. She accepted the apology, and I thanked her and told her how grateful I was that the Lord allowed the picture to draw us together for this moment of healing. She was amazed as well. God cares about the healing of offenses and will line up opportunities to bring forgiveness forward.

Praise His name!

"Do all the good you can. By all the means you can. In all the places you can. At all the times you can. As long as ever you can."

John Wesley

CHAPTER 10

Power in Praise and Worship

"Let everything that has breath, praise the Lord. Praise the Lord!" (Psalm 150:6) The Lord is seeking those who will worship Him in spirit and in truth. The Lord inhabits (lives in) the praises of His people. Praise is the open door or gateway to worship. The Lord loves it when we sing to Him. Whether it be the hymns of old or the current songs, as our songs magnify Him, He is pleased to hear them. Praising the Lord in song lifts your spirit and helps you to get your eyes off of yourself and onto Him and His majestic power, glory, and love. Praise is also a weapon of prayer that releases judgment on the enemy, as the Bible says that praise will bind kings.

> *Let them praise His name with the dance; Let them sing praises to Him with the timbrel and harp. For the Lord takes pleasure in His people; He will beautify the humble with salvation. Let the saints*

be joyful in glory; let them sing aloud on their beds.
Let the high praises of God be in their mouth, and
a two-edged sword in their hand, to execute ven-
geance on the nations, And punishments on the
peoples; To bind their kings with chains, and their
nobles with fetters of iron; To execute on them the
written judgment, this honor have all His saints.
Praise the Lord!

Psalm 149:3-9

Praise is the gateway into worship, and worship will open the door for you to draw near to the heart of the Lord. Remember Satan in the wilderness tempting Jesus.

The final temptation he offered Jesus was all the kingdoms of the world and all his authority he would give Him if he would do one thing, bow down and worship him (Luke 4:5-7). True worship will allow you entry into His presence, where He will cause you to be filled with the fragrance of His beauty. When your humbled heart begins to seek His face, He will respond to you, and many times, release great revelation to you of His love and glory. Worship allows you the ability to move past the outer courts of the flesh and into the Holy of holies, where the veil of flesh is removed, and we truly behold Him.

Obedience Produces His Trust in You

"Has the Lord as great delight in burnt offerings and sacrifices, as in obeying the voice of the Lord? Behold to obey is better than sacrifice, And to heed than the fat of rams. For rebellion is as the sin of witchcraft, and stubbornness is as iniquity and idolatry" (1 Samuel 15:22-23). The Lord desires our obedience more than any of our sacrifices. Obedience to whatever He says to do will produce a great trust the Lord will have in you. This obedience will also release the blessing and increase in your life. *"If you are willing and obedient, you shall eat the good of the land"* (Isaiah 1:19). Many times, the things He will tell you to do will make no sense in the natural, but after you've obeyed, you will see why He sent you, and it is such a rewarding moment to know you collaborated with the King of glory, amen. He releases blessings to you as you obey Him.

Release His Kingdom Authority

"Behold, I give you the authority to trample on serpents and scorpions, and over all the power of the enemy, and nothing shall by in any means hurt you" (Luke 10:19). We need to stand in the authority that He has given us and realize that the God who lives within us is greater than any demonic spirit coming against us. We have the power to overcome Satan by the blood of the Lamb and the word of our testimony. We need to apply and practice these truths in our daily life. The blood of Jesus Christ

has been released over this world when He shed it at His death. It contains such power that whenever it is mentioned during prayer, especially prayers for deliverance, the enemy gives up as he knows that the blood defeated him. We, as the body of Christ, need to know about and operate in our authority.

A few years after I was saved, I was asked to stay overnight at a family member's home while they went out of town. I was the only one in the house, and the television was left on as I fell asleep. At around 3 a.m., I woke up and sensed a fearful presence in the room. Standing next to the television was a demonic being (I believe it was Satan) staring at me with jet black hair slicked back and dark eyes filled with such hatred, and I knew it wanted to murder me. I cannot accurately describe the fear that overwhelmed me in that room. All of a sudden, I felt a very strong presence within me rising up from my belly, and out of my mouth came these words, "The blood of Jesus," and the spirit vanished instantly and never returned. We have authority over all the power of the enemy, and we need to know this truth and apply it to our lives, amen.

"We need never shout across the spaces to an absent God. He is nearer than our own soul, closer than our most secret thoughts."

A.W. Tozer

CHAPTER 11

Lose Control

In this journey to wholeness, control is a very difficult spirit to break free from. You see, not even the Lord controls us. He leads us ever so gently down His pathway of wisdom, peace, and joy in His shepherd-like way, but He will only lead you if you are willing to allow Him to have the control panel of your life.

Let the wicked forsake his way, and the unrighteous man his thoughts; Let him return to the Lord, and He will have mercy on him; and to our God, for He will abundantly pardon. "For My thoughts are not your thoughts, nor are your ways My ways," says the Lord. For as the heavens are higher than the earth, so are My ways higher than your ways, and My thoughts than your thoughts.

Isaiah 55:7-9

Control is witchcraft. It is the highest form of pride because the Lord is not allowed to lead or guide you, and that makes you a God unto yourself, or someone else has become your God or idol. Several years ago, I had a traumatic encounter with a Jezebel spirit which almost took my life. I release my testimony to you only to help you see the depths of control and the power of Jesus Christ, who sets the captives free. Remember that we do not battle flesh and blood, and people are not our enemies. I title this testimony "The Great Escape from Jezebel."

The spirit of Jezebel is in the church. In Revelation 2:18-28, there is a warning about permitting the spirit of Jezebel to operate in the church.

> "And to the Angel of the church in Thyatira write, 'These things says the Son of God, who has eyes like a flame of fire, and His feet like fine brass: I know your works, love, service, faith, and your patience; and as for your works, the last are more than the first. Nevertheless, I have a few things against you, because you allow that woman Jezebel, who calls herself a prophetess, to teach and seduce My servants to commit sexual immorality and eat things sacrificed to idols. And I gave her time to repent of her sexual immorality and she did not repent. Indeed I will cast her into a sickbed, and those who commit adultery with her into great tribulation, unless they repent of their deeds. I will kill her chil-

*dren with death, and all the churches shall know
that I am He who searches the minds and hearts.
And I will give to each one of you according to your
works. Now to you I say, and to the rest in Thyatira,
as many as do not have this doctrine, who have not
known the depths of Satan, as they say, I will put on
you no other burden. But hold fast what you have
till I come. And he who overcomes, and keeps My
works until the end, to him I will give power over
the nations. "He shall rule them with a rod of iron;
They shall be dashed to pieces like the potter's ves-
sels"; as I also have received from My Father, and I
will give him the morning star.'"*

The church is perishing because of a lack of knowledge. *"And they overcame him [Satan] by the blood of the
Lamb and the word of their testimony, and they did not love
their lives to the death"* (Revelation 12:11).

This testimony will hopefully prevent you from becoming her next victim. The Lord takes the pain and
suffering you live through, and when He heals you and
delivers you, He anoints you, so you reach out to others
who hurt the same way, and they cry out for answers.
Jezebel was the wife of Ahab, king of Israel. She was a
worshiper of Baal (a false god and an idol) and had her
four hundred prophets who followed her. She controlled
Ahab and basically made all the decisions over Israel

during his reign. She was a murderer of the prophets of the Most High God. During a time of severe famine, Elijah, the prophet, was sent to Ahab to confront his idolatrous lifestyle. There was a showdown between Elijah and the four hundred prophets of Baal to prove who was indeed the only true God.

The Lord consumed Elijah's sacrifice of wood soaked in water and proved His mighty power as the wood ignites with a heavenly flame. All the prophets of Baal were slain. Jezebel became murderous and wanted revenge on Elijah. Her intimidation was so strong that Elijah ran and hid from her in a cave. Jehu, the conqueror, finally defeated her when she was thrown out of a window to her death and eaten by dogs according to the word of the Lord. Although she died, the spirits that operated through her didn't. They are still here on this earth but will one day be thrown into the Lake of Fire with Satan. The spirit of Jezebel is assigned to abort the plan of God in a region or territory.

The spirit of Elijah is being released in this hour for the restoring of the hearts of the fathers to the children and the children to the fathers as it was spoken through the prophet Malachi. Jezebel wants to prevent this from happening by seducing the church through idolatry and witchcraft. The church must rise up and confront this stronghold through prayer, then face to face. (I will refer to this spirit as a her, but it can operate in a man as well.) The first way the spirit operates is through a flattering tongue, "Oh, you have such a mighty anointing, and you are so needed in the church. Why haven't they recognized you? Your gift is not being used." Proverbs 29:5 states, "A man who flatters his neighbor spreads a net for his feet." A trap or snare is set up. The purpose of the flattery is to gain the person's trust. Please do not confuse flattery with giving honor where it is due. Jezebel will expound on your great anointing and may even release a prophetic word. The gifting of the prophetic actually operates through her, but she is not spiritually connected to the Holy Spirit. She speaks through a familiar spirit, similar to the psychics, and these familiar spirits have studied you all your life. Romans 11:29 states, "For the gifts and calling of God are irrevocable." The prophetic word should edify, build up, and many times confirm what the Lord has already spoken to you. Every prophetic word needs to be judged by your pastor or covering, who will help you rightly divide that word, and if it's truly from the Lord, it will come to pass. It was the Lord's governmental plan to install apostles, prophets, pastors, teachers, and evangelists for the equipping and training of the church. Jezebel is a seductress and knows the exact words to speak to her victim to gain control. She may appear as a very sweet and holy person, or she may be purely judgmental.

We need to be spiritual fruit inspectors and know those who labor among us. Matthew 7:16 states, *"You will know them by their fruits."* The easiest way to recognize Jezebel is through her dominating control and manipulation. You may find it very difficult to say no to her. Any person who imposes their will upon another is operating in witchcraft. Any person who prays their own will or desire for another, rather than the Lord's will, is also operating in witchcraft. This spirit loves to catch you off guard. It will take control over anyone that gives it permission. Jezebel loves to get a "rise" out of her victims. She'll cross personal boundaries any way she pleases in a very smooth and quick manner. It is absolutely shocking the things said and done by her. Remember that Satan pushes, and the Lord leads. This spirit, not dealt with, will move into your home, church, or job and take over any way it sees fit. Remember you must be the keeper of your heart at all times, for out of it spring the issues of life (Proverbs 4:23).

This spirit can be very religious; as a matter of fact, Jezebel drives her victims to pray longer than most ministers. She will pray an entire day, as no sacrifice is too great, including family or any other responsibility. She loves to attend prayer meetings of any kind with an agenda to control them. She's usually the one who prays the longest and sometimes the loudest. The Jezebel spirit works with the spirit of divination, which is mentioned in Acts 16:16.

Divination operates in fortune-tellers, gypsies, psychics, etc., for monetary gain, and the Apostle Paul dealt with it on the way to prayer. This spirit knows how to seduce money out of others, using her controlling powers. She also knows the Bible very well, reading for hours and hours. She calls herself a prophetess. This is why it is so hard to recognize her. There is very strong legalism that operates through her. She is extremely judgmental and is always pointing out the faults of others. She explains that this is a special commission by God to judge others.

She operates in false humility and a victim mentality. She uses the term "deep" quite often, referring to deep, deep teachings or revelations given only to her. Sometimes they are so deep they cause confusion. The teaching we give or receive must line up with God's word; if it doesn't line up, throw it out. This spirit thrives on power and authority. She refuses to submit to any spiritual authority, as she believes she has been ordained by God to be her own covering, accountable to no one. Because of the severe wounding of heart, she feels misunderstood by many in authority and isolates herself to serve God under isolation. Jezebel is a spiritual abuser, and she doesn't care who she wounds. Her purpose is to steal prophetic mantles and convince you that she is the only one who is truly holy and hears from God for her and you.

She becomes, therefore, an idol to you because you have to check with her on everything spiritual to make sure you are correct. Before long, you can't operate spiritually at all without her help, and now you are under her full control. This lying spirit convinces you that anyone attempting to disagree with her is from Satan and is in error. Meanwhile, the victim under her influence, control, or "spell" is separated from all other influences, especially those Elijahs who speak the truth and expose her. If she does not attain the position of power and authority, she will leave and blame them for "missing out on God's visitation." She'll quietly leave the church and plant seeds of division, so the church splits, and then she starts attacking a new victim. The judgments spoken about others are continual; she is always pointing the finger at others and devaluing them. Psalm 1:1 says, *"Blessed is the man who walks not in the counsel of the ungodly, nor stands in the path of sinners, nor sits in the seat of the scornful."*

This spirit will identify itself through these actions, as well as perfectionism, and will attempt to train you to act just like her, like her offspring. No one seemingly can measure up to her as she has no faults. It is always someone else with the problem. Spiritual pride (Baal) is the strong man over this spirit. The fruit from a relationship with Jezebel is fear, intimidation, guilt, self-condemnation, no self-control, no self-worth, and no compassion. There is a proper balance to everything we do as Christians. We must learn to say no and establish spiritual boundaries around us. The easiest of her preys are wounded and rejected Christians, abused, divorced, widowed, fatherless, and those who operate in a strong mercy gift.

Zechariah 7:10 says, "*Do not oppress the widow or the fatherless, the alien or the poor.*" The spirit needs to have an Ahab to control, and through her seductions, she convinces her victims she genuinely cares about them. Actually, they are ensnared by her, and only by the grace of the Lord can her victims escape from her.

My Day of Deliverance

Twenty years ago, I was one of Jezebel's victims, and through the power of truth, anointed prayer, and fasting, I can testify that I have escaped her control. I met her at a prayer meeting at a job. She spoke flattering words to me and seemed very caring. The Word says in Proverbs 26:28, "*A lying tongue hates those who are crushed by it and a flattering mouth works ruin.*" The snare came when she spoke a false prophetic word over me, which overwhelmed me to hear a "word" spoken from God to me. I was not familiar with prophetic words and never saw gifts like that operating in anyone like that before.

All I desired was to get closer to God any way I could, so I was elated that God would send someone to release a direct word to me and that someone would be willing to spend time with me to show me how to get closer to Him.

Over a period of time, I was consumed with half the daily prayer times, more time with God than with anyone else, including my two beautiful daughters that I was raising and now had no time for. I knew something was way out of balance, but I overlooked it, as she controlled me and intimidated me, convincing me this was God's will for me. Before long, I cut off my family, church, and all friends for the sake of the anointing. I would have to forsake all as Abraham did. The result? I left my pastoral covering and allowed her to be my covering, living under her control and spell. Because of my love for the Lord, I am convinced He extended grace to me to endure this trial. Praise God for my caring and praying sister, who saw the extreme control and listened to the Lord to fast and pray for my freedom from this spirit's control.

I received a phone call from a friend who had gone to a Mario Murillo conference with her husband. When they went forward for prayer for their marriage, Mario told her a Jezebel spirit was coming against them to destroy their marriage and ministry, and he broke the spirit off of her. She was calling to warn me to get away from this person as fast as I could. I found it hard to accept what she said, but the seed of my deliverance had gone into my soul through that phone call. My girls were so angry that their mother was under this control and begged me to get away and be their mother again.

My sister was praying at home. The following Sunday morning, I woke up with the most painful stiff neck as I left the patio window open a crack to cool down. I couldn't move my head even an inch without pain. Three times the Lord said to go back to my church for service, and I told my daughter she would have to be my side mirror for me in the car. My neck was injured in a fall about a month before at work. We had to sit in the balcony, as the place was packed.

The worship began, and the anointing was powerful in that place. Then, the pastor stopped and began to quote Psalm 91, which happened to be my favorite psalm. I knew it almost by heart, so I spoke it with him as I closed my eyes, and the anointing (tangible presence) of the Lord was so strong, I literally saw the presence of the Lord in front of me. I began to feel such peace as the word was spoken.

The pastor then shouted, "Someone in the balcony is being healed of a neck problem. Move it." I tried to move my head, but the pain was still so intense. I began to thank the Lord for healing that person even though it wasn't me. About a minute later, he said it again, "You,

in the balcony, with the neck problem, keep moving
it." After five tries, I noticed the pain began to slowly
leave, and then it was gone completely! I could move my
neck back and forth with no pain whatsoever. I began to
thank Jesus. The pastor said, "Get down here and testify
if the Lord has touched you." I ran out of my seat and
down the stairs as quickly as I could as I knew the Lord
had touched me. When the pastor laid hands on me, it
was like I got struck by lightning.

I came off that floor flooded with peace and joy.
When I got home, I discovered another miracle had
taken place; my eyes were opened, and Jezebel's spell
had been broken off of me! I knew that I had to get
away from her quickly. I also knew I had to confront her
and explain what God had done for me and showed me
about being around her and that I was leaving. Anyone
who confronts this spirit is immediately the enemy, but
it was a small price for the freedom received. I pray for
this person as often as the Lord leads me to, and for
many years, I wondered why I would have to go through
such a painful experience, but now I understand why,
as I have helped hundreds get free from this controlling
spirit and stay free, amen.

Ask yourself these questions:

- Who is this person, and did God send them into
  my life to encourage me or hinder me?

- Does this person control me, and do I need to check with them before I make decisions?
- Do I feel pressure to do what I really don't want to do whenever they are around? Then feel guilty for saying no?
- Am I in possession of my own will, or have I given it to someone else?
- Do I feel condemned when I don't pray or read the Word for at least one hour per day?
- Do I feel like I need someone to hear from God for me?
- Do I feel nervous or intimidated around certain people, and I can't be myself?
- Do I keep company with faultfinders and find myself becoming critical and judgmental of others?
- Do I try to avoid this person when I see them coming toward me?
- Can I pray for you?

If you answered yes to any of the questions above, then you may be under the influence of the Jezebel spirit (actually the spirit of Baal, who she served). The pathway to deliverance is repentance. If you are the person I described in the testimony and you have been acting that way toward others, Jesus can set you free right now. *"If My people who are called by My name will humble them-*

selves, and pray and seek My face, and turn from their wicked ways, then I will hear from heaven, forgive their sin and heal their land" (2 Chronicles 7:14).

The land healed will be yours! Maybe you are the one in control in your home, and it is filled with arguing and strife. The enemy uses deception and ignorance of spiritual things, and we don't want to be ignorant of Satan and his devices. Jesus said, *"The thief does not come except to steal, and to kill, and to destroy. I have come that they may have life, and that they may have it more abundantly"* (John 10:10).

I want to help you to sever all ties to this strongman spirit and give Jesus the place He so rightly deserves. Baal is the strongman over America, and we can take authority over it and command it to get out of our lives and pray for our families as we share the revelation with them. Together in unity, we can drive this spirit out, once and for all.

Let's pray: "Father, in the name of Jesus, I now recognize the Jezebel spirit's influence over my life. Father, I repent for coming under its influence in any way, and I choose to turn from it and renounce witchcraft and control in my life completely in Jesus' name. I make a choice today to divorce the spirit of Baal, who Jezebel served, and I decree and declare deliverance from all sexual immorality and idolatry. I choose to serve and follow the Lord Jesus Christ in every area of my life.

Set me free, Lord, from every spirit that is associated with Baal. I recommit my life to You, Jesus, to love You. I declare Your lordship over every area of my life, spirit, soul, and body in Jesus' mighty name, amen."

I pray for you who prayed that prayer: "Father, I command the spirit of Baal, Jezebel, and Leviathan (the king over all the children of pride) to leave this person now in Jesus' mighty name. You are now trespassing on holy ground that is no longer yours! Loose them now and leave! Father, cover them with the precious holy blood of Jesus from head to toes. That blood has purchased their deliverance from all evil. Father, shut and seal every doorway to these demonic spirits, and I ask for warring angels to go forth and bring back everything that enemy stole from them with sevenfold interest in Jesus' name, amen." Be free.

"Let God's promises shine on your problems."

Corrie Ten Boom

CHAPTER 12

Abuser vs. Abused. The Verdict

Many years ago, I helped my friend and mentor, Theresa Duffy, write a short testimony booklet titled Abuse, Breaking the Curse. Theresa and I served as team leaders at our church, the Rock of Sarasota, in the 1990s. Our pastor, Richard Brantley, saw a great need for his church and others who needed additional prayer for healing and deliverance. Pastor called it Set Free Ministries. This ministry went on for seven years, and we witnessed the Lord setting His people free from lifelong sin, and through the power of Jesus' name, bondages were removed from the people. Two of the most prayed over bondages we encountered were the spirit of abuse and the spirit of offense.

They operated together as a team. The offended were many times abused, and some even became abusers, and the abused were all offended, and some wanted vengeance. In 2001, we were invited to speak at a Women's Aglow meeting to share our testimonies. The Aglow president invited all of the area Aglow leaders to hear us and receive prayer for their lives. There were approximately ninety pastors' wives who attended from all over the state. In one particular meeting, we had no idea what God was about to do, and I have to say I had never seen anything like it. The best way to describe the meeting was that God peeled back a veil that was covering each of those precious women, and He exposed their hearts before them.

Everyone forgave the people they held unforgiveness toward for years. One woman stated, in tears, that she held hatred toward her husband for forty-five years because he danced with a woman at their wedding, and after the testimony on offense, she went and called him to ask for forgiveness. When Theresa shared her testimony on abuse and began to pray for the women, it was like a whirlwind entered the place, and women fell out of their chairs, and the Holy Spirit set them free, one by one, as she broke the curse of abuse off of their lives and then the children's lives. I will never forget that incredible move of the Holy Spirit!

Recently, while in prayer, the Lord laid on my heart to release Theresa's personal testimony in a courtroom scene. Theresa takes the stand as the witness. The others present in the courtroom are the Judge, the prosecuting attorney, the defense attorney, and the abuser (plaintiff).

This is a reenactment of what takes place before the throne of God.

One of the most difficult subjects to discuss is abuse. Every living being has been exposed to this subject. I don't care what level of society they reside in or how perfectly they were raised, they have been exposed to it or they are actively involved in it every day of their life. Regardless of how much exposure there has been in our lives, the truth is this secret sin has been operating in our families, churches, and non-religious society since the very beginning of creation.

Definition of "abuse": "to treat a person or animal with cruelty or violence, especially regularly or repeatedly." Statistics will startle you. On average, nearly twenty people per minute are physically abused by an intimate partner in the United States. During one year, this equates to more than ten million men and women. One in four men and one in three women. (Taken from the National Coalition Against Domestic Violence.)

There are several categories of abuse:

- physical (domestic violence, narcissism)
- emotional (mental, trauma, PTSD)
- sexual (rape, sex traffic, incest)

- spiritual (ritual abuse, spiritual control through fear)
- verbal (destructive and threatening words)

Before you begin to read this book, the Lord wants me to look you right in your eyes (with His eyes) and speak this powerful message from His heart to both the abuser and the abused: "My beloved one, you're never alone; someone cares for you more than you've known; someone loves you just the way you are; you don't have to change who I made you to be. I hear your cries, I see your fears, and I came to deliver you and set you free. Jesus"

The Judge is about to enter this courtroom: *will all rise!*

The Prosecuting Attorney Speaks: "Your Honor, Before You Stands an Abuser"

In my research to discover the motivating purpose for someone who desires to do harm or injure another individual who is created in God's image, I discovered several common patterns that I need to present before this court.

This man (or woman) has been witnessed committing the following crimes:

He's unable to hold back his temper, becoming enraged with his victims.

He lifts his hand or even a weapon to his victims to cause physical harm to them.

He screams at his victims to demonstrate his power and control.

He ridicules them at will to destroy their self-worth and self-confidence.

He corrects them in public, bringing embarrassment to them.

He threatens to do harm to them if they tell anyone about his behavior.

He causes his victims to isolate themselves from friends and family.

He bullies them and harasses them emotionally, spiritually, or sexually.

He pridefully demands that all attention be drawn to him, never others.

He entraps them financially so they cannot leave and threatens them with fear they won't survive without him.

He lies about his hidden life consisting of all sorts of depravity and secret sin.

He causes his victims to "walk on eggshells," never knowing when he will explode.

He uses the Bible as a weapon to accuse and blame all his behavior on his victim and others.

This abuser, many times, will meditate on ending his own life and suffers from severe mental depression. My client (nameless) became his defenseless victim and married him, desiring to be loved and provided for in a happy and safe home, have mutual respect, but was deceived by a masked prince charming when this person came along. If someone could just reach into his heart and pull out all the bitterness, control, anger, and jealousy, they'd be able to actually live a peaceful and happy life together. Your Honor, I submit to this court that this human being is hopeless, evil, a threat to our society and to himself. I am asking the court to place him in prison and keep him locked away so he can no longer harm another person. This individual will remain this way for the rest of his life, and there is nothing that will ever change him. Your Honor, I am requesting the harshest punishment of the law. The prosecution rests.

Defense Attorney Speaks Defending the Abuser

Your Honor, the charges filed against my client are many. I represented him because of his cries for help, and no one else cared to advise or listen to him. You see, my client did not wake up one day and decide He was going to abuse or hurt someone. He needed someone to talk to, a pastor, a counselor, a mentor, a trained listening ear who could help him to live a normal healthy life. The guilt and shame from his past kept this family problem a secret. He remembers the family threat, "If you dare to mention to anyone else about this, you will certainly pay." You see, when he was a child, he was constantly abused by his father, who also suffered abuse from his upbringing.

Because of the indescribable trauma my client endured through his childhood, he became emotionally damaged and endured constant rejection, and it produced bitterness. His dad could not handle normal everyday life problems. His condition caused him to have sudden outbursts of rage, and my client bore some of his hardest blows. Why doesn't my dad love me? Why did he have kids to treat them this way? If that wasn't bad enough, he was beaten up at school several times by a bully that would single him out. He was always in trouble at school. He didn't pay attention in class and was always called out and ridiculed for being the school troublemaker.

He was an outcast, labeled as a troublemaker. Abused at home, abused at school. Finally, he had enough of the abuse, and his only recourse was to leave the abuse somehow. He would hear voices in his head telling him, You are a useless human being. *Nobody cares about you. Why don't you just end your life?* He thought about taking his life several times, but fear of death and where he would end up kept him from that drastic and terrifying decision. Can you even imagine the fear, the rejection, the shame, and the guilt that followed him all his life? He never encountered a normal family life; that was only a dream. Then, one night, he met her, Sarah, the love of his life.

She was beautiful and so nice, so encouraging to him. He was drawn to her immediately. He was ashamed to tell her about his awful past, so he never opened up to her in fear of losing her. After just one month of spending time with her, he asked her to marry him. To his shock, she said yes. Things went well in the beginning, but when they began to argue, he couldn't control the rage inside. Sarah was shocked, "Who is this other person I said 'I do' to at our wedding? This is not a marriage but a personal massacre." Then, as the arguing increased and Sarah voiced her disappointment and sorrow that she ever met him, she struck a deep-seeded nerve in his heart that confirmed he was planted in his past; she repeated what he was always told, "You are useless, a failure, a mistake!" Those words shattered him to the core of his soul, and he reacted in rage; he began to physically push her, slap her, and threaten her.

He was out of control. It was his childhood all over again. She finally left him for good. He called and begged her to forgive him and said he would never do it again and that he needed her. She was the only person who ever understood him. She refused and would never permit him back into her life. He remembered those voices again and agreed he was useless. He now faces charges that will destroy his life and ability to work if he is convicted by this court. He has never remarried, so this will not happen again, he promises.

Your Honor, he is asking for the mercy of the court. He never expected his life to be just like his dad's, and he asks for forgiveness for all his wrongdoings. He is seeking spiritual counseling with his pastor in order to fully recover from this emotional trauma and, most importantly, to remove this dangerous generational pattern from his life. May I suggest that an updated report be given to this court by his pastor, which explains my client's progress in six months? This pastor seems to think that the God he believes in has the ability to help my client through all of this and bring some sort of healing to his soul and break this cycle of abuse off of his life.

The defense rests.

A Witness Testifies

We call to the stand, Your Honor, Theresa Duffy, who will be a witness to this court of the reality and the results of being trapped inside of an abusive home. She has courageously agreed to testify her true-life story, to shine the light of truth over this tragic behavior and its severe consequences upon everyone who lived in this home environment. As this court will clearly see, there is only one who can help someone who is locked in this horrible prison cell. If I may, I want to begin with a word from Theresa's local pastor:

> "Silent prisoners of war," Theresa has correctly labeled, as the throngs of humanity go hopelessly trudging along, blindly unaware that there is a way out! Hallelujah! Before your very eyes and in your own hands, you hold a recipe for deliverance. By taking the Word of God, applying its time-tested, Holy-Spirit-anointed truths to every area of her life, and by systematically walking faithfully alongside divinely placed pastoral covering, as her pastor, I have had the joy and pleasure of observing Theresa's full recovery.
>
> I would encourage you now to tenaciously follow what you are about to read, learning to remove what Theresa calls "tombstone talk" from your very vocabulary, and unflinchingly, immediately, begin to put these proven principles to work, step by step. Please afford me the privilege to pray with you as you begin, "Heavenly Father, I ask You to cocoon and anoint the reader of this book in Your protective care and open the eyes of their heart so that they may enjoy a clear understanding of all that You have inspired Theresa to write.

Resulting in, Father, a full surrender to Your Majesty, trusting in Your deliverance, and complete recovery from the damage of their past. I ask You this and thank You, in the precious name of Your Son, Jesus Christ our Lord, amen."

In His service,

Richard L. Brantley

Senior Pastor, the Rock of Sarasota

Sarasota, Florida"

Your Honor, millions of people live in abuse as victims for years, not knowing that it is a generational curse. Abuse victims are silent "prisoners of war" with usually no hope for a way out. They just put up with it. Abuse is familiar and tolerated by many for years as a way of life. The devastation that passes down to the next generation, unless stopped, will increase to a greater capacity. The good news is that there is a way out of abuse. Millions cry before the throne of God for help. I was one of those millions who cried out for twenty years. Through divine revelation, God gave me the answer I needed to break loose from its deadly cycle.

Taking the Word of God and applying the truth found therein to your life will evidence a change. These principles have been shared with many, and the results are proven and immediate. Be encouraged; abuse can be stopped. *My testimony*: The Lord established families as the authority on this earth. Families that know and honor the Word of God will, through knowledge, speak life to their children and establish them on His chosen path. If you are ignorant of the Word, then you could be used by the dark kingdom to speak words of death that will destroy their path in life and pull them off their divine destiny. As a child, my worth was never discussed, but my unworthiness was. My father spoke words of death over me out of ignorance.

Words we take into our ear gate, like food in our mouth, are digested into our spirit and soul. "Death and life are in the power of the tongue, and those who love it will eat its fruit." What you meditate on is what you become, and I reran the words my father spoke until they became flesh. The fruit I was eating was rotten. My family did not realize that what they were saying were seeds. The words he spoke produced a curse upon my life, and I was bound by those words. A stronghold was formed over my mind where I could not believe anything except the spoken words. This stronghold, which was a lie, became a fortress, and I could not perceive myself in any other light. Raised in a denominational church, I attended a parochial school, which did not encourage us to read the Bible. In fact, it discouraged it, and due to this, I was illiterate in this area.

We were given books to read and taught to love and revere God. This I did. My family was faithful to do those things prescribed by the church we belonged to. God's word states, "My people perish for lack of knowledge," and I lacked true knowledge of Him and His will for my life.

The future road ahead of me was destructive. My children and I were perishing through the pain and sorrow we suffered. Every relationship in my life was affected by this lie. The spirit of abuse that I was now familiar with would draw me to seek those who would abuse me. It was not unlikely that my choice for a spouse would be one who was familiar with abuse. Around the fourth year of my marriage, our family encountered multiple tragedies. There was a death of a family member, a severe illness, and other misfortunes. We always thought that God helps those who help themselves. This, of course, is not biblical. The abuse in my home escalated due to the tragedies. The destructive poison of abusive words now had produced lesions in my spirit and soul, which needed healing. By now, I had three children, and the rage and abusive words affected each of them. *Perhaps*, I thought, *if there were a new setting, a move away, or leave for a different place, things might just change.* After ten years of marriage and living in New York, we packed up our belongings and moved to Florida, knowing nothing about demons at that time.

I was clueless that they were also moving to Florida. I'm sure they helped us pack. Every time I put my key in the door, I would say, "I'm going into hell." Of course, that was where I was going. The kingdom of darkness was established and operating in my home. I had prophesied it over myself without knowing it. If there is abuse operating in the home or on the job, it is not of God. "Please, help me!" I cried out to the Lord. I thought God had forgotten about me because nothing had changed. As a matter of fact, it grew worse every day. We kept our home in New York, where we would spend the summers. In the town was a little country library where I would go to check out books. I remember a display of books on the counter written by Chuck Colson and Billy Graham about being "born again." I did not like that expression, "born again," so I ignored those books. I didn't know what it meant to be born again. Something inside of me did not like it. There was a book that caught my eye sitting on a table called *The Helper* by Catherine Marshall. Desperately needing help, I chose that book and took it by the lake to read. It was all about the Holy Spirit being our helper. With my background in a traditional church, I didn't know the office of the Holy Spirit or what His role was in the Trinity. All I knew was He was part of the Trinity: Father, Son, and Holy Ghost. At the end of each chapter of that book, Catherine Marshall would include scripture from the book of John.

Every time I read those scriptures, I wept because they were reaching right inside my heart. I thought to myself, *My goodness, how beautiful that God loves me. I never knew that.* The God I was taught about was far away from me and unapproachable. Often, I would go to God through others, such as His mother and the saints.

The author went on to say, "If you want this Holy Spirit, you can ask Him to come into your life, and He will take over. He will take your sin, pain, and sorrow." I was so glad to give Him my sorrow, and it was so easy to receive Him. Putting down my book, I bowed my head and confessed with my mouth, "Dear Lord, I repent of my sin. Please take my pain, sorrow, and grief. I invite You into my life and thank You for taking it over." Returning to Florida, I picked up a church bulletin, where I read about a seven-week seminar entitled "Life in the Spirit" that was being held each Friday. At the end of seven weeks, the leader gathered the group together and prayed for us to receive the baptism of the Holy Spirit, and I spoke in tongues. When I realized that the Bible was God's love letter, I personalized it. The spirit of God then became my instructor.

As I started to read the Bible, I realized that in John 3:3, Jesus was the one who said, *"You must be born again."* The chapter of Mark 16:15 was one the Holy Spirit kept me in for quite some time until the rhema (a God quickened word) reached down into my spirit, and as I acted out on the Word, it then became flesh, and a foundation was laid in my spirit. Jesus said in Mark 16:15 (the Great Commission), *"Go into all the world and preach the gospel to every creature."* I wanted to be obedient to everything Jesus said and was determined that I would believe only what was written in His Word and act on it. I began to reach out to others and study His Word every day.

In Mark 16:16, Jesus states, *"He who believes and is baptized will be saved; but he who does not believe will be condemned."* Thinking back to my baptism as an infant, I realized that the decision was not mine to make. I resolved to be obedient and be baptized and now had the understanding that when I went under the water, I died to myself with Christ, and as I rose out of the water, I was resurrected with Him.

In Mark 16:17, the Holy Spirit showed me that signs always follow a believer.

First sign: in My name, they will cast out demons.

Second sign: they will speak with new tongues.

Third sign: they will take up serpents, and if they drink of any deadly, it will by no means hurt them.

Fourth sign: they will lay hands on the sick, and they will recover. After Jesus said that, He was received up into heaven and sat at the right hand of God. Reading this, I thought to myself how important those words were. They were the last words Jesus spoke to His apostles before leaving this earth. I knew I had to be obedient to step out and do the works of the believer. The Holy Spirit told me that verse 20 was a key scripture for the above signs. It states, *"And they went out and preached everywhere, the Lord working with them and confirming the word through accompanying signs."*

He, the Holy Spirit, said, "It is not what I (Theresa) say or the pastor or the church but only what the Word states will Jesus confirm." I was not walking in all these signs as of yet. I had not accomplished the first sign; I never cast out a demon, and since it is in the Word, I told the Holy Spirit I would definitely do it; I just had to find a demon. The next sign mentioned is "they will speak with new tongues." I checked that one off because Jesus had baptized me with the evidence of speaking in tongues. The third sign is "they will take up serpents, and if they drink anything deadly, it will by no means hurt them," and the last sign is "they will lay hands on the sick, and they will recover." I now knew I had to lay hands on the sick and cast out a demon.

One night, my young son called me and asked me to rub his legs because of pain; this happened quite often. As I was rubbing his legs and telling him what I learned in the Bible, that God heals and delivers, he said to me, "Well, if God heals, then tell Him to heal my legs!" For a split second, I thought, *If this doesn't work, my son will never believe,* but my next thought was that this was a "Holy Spirit opportunity" to prove that Word works. I laid my hands on his legs and said a short prayer, and the pain instantly left. He jumped up with delight, and I left the room praising the Lord for God's faithfulness. The next checklist item was to cast out a demon and, living in a house of abuse, I did not have to go far to find one. There were many around me.

Passing the den one day, I saw my son lying on the couch coiled in a fetal position. I perceived this to be the spirit of fear and asked my son to come into his bedroom. Obediently, he came in and sat on his bed, and I spoke to the demon and said, "You, spirit of fear, come out of my son in the name of Jesus." There was a small radio by the side of the bed, which made a blast. Both my son and I jumped back. James said, "Mom, I feel so much better; something has lifted from me."

To complete my checklist, I knew not to pick up serpents, but if I did, I could brush it off and say, "Be healed in the name of Jesus." I was able to complete the last sign when my friend called to tell me she had cancer. While undergoing chemotherapy (which is poison to the body), she was unable to keep any food down. The Lord gave me the word in Mark 16:18; it states, *"...if they drink anything deadly, it will by no means hurt them..."* After praying with her in agreement, she was able to eat and keep her food down. Although this was not an instant healing, we had a lot to learn about perseverance, believing, and standing on the Word. Activating her own faith in the Word healed her.

The word of God works if we believe and act on it.

I joined a Bible study in order to grow in the Word. The Word released my inner man and washed the error out, bringing in truth. As I acted upon the knowledge I was receiving, God empowered me to walk with signs following. Within my home, abuse was still ruling and reigning. How could this be? The Word worked, and it was proven over and over again in every area but abuse. I was confused. I sought counsel to stop the abuse, and as a woman of the Word, I stood upon the scriptures that they gave me. First Peter 3:1 states, *"Wives, likewise, be submissive to your own husbands, that even if some do not obey the word, they, without a word, may be won by the conduct of their wives."* First Peter 3:4 states, *"With the incorruptible beauty of a gentle and quiet spirit, which is very precious in the sight of God."* Ephesians 5:23 states, *"For the husband is the head of the wife, as also Christ is the head of the church; and He is the Savior of the body."* I stood on these words, and I prayed them and fasted, but the abuse continued. What was the stumbling block? I continued to cry out to God. As the years passed, the abuse was still in operation in my home. My children had become victims as well.

Your children are not immune because *what you allow is what you teach.*

The curse, unless stopped, will continue down to the next generation. No longer able to go on, I packed my clothes. I called a friend who offered to let me stay with her. Alone in my friend's home, I walked around her living room, screaming out to God. "What kind of God are You to let me suffer for years, and You never did anything? You could have stopped it, but because I know what a mighty God You are, I guess You just chose not to."

I heard the audible voice of the Lord, and He said, "Whatever you allow on earth is allowed in heaven."

He showed me a vision of two kingdoms, the kingdom of God and the kingdom of Satan. I saw myself in Satan's kingdom, down on my knees with my hands raised, worshiping him, and I screamed out, "It's my fault?"

Just then, my friend walked in, and I asked her if I could lie down. I slept for two days, and when I awoke, I knew I had to leave. I did not discuss with her what God said or the vision. God had spoken; I did not want to hear from man's counsel. Your Honor, the curse of abuse can be broken, regardless of how many generations have passed by. The Word of God contains the answer to every sin problem we face if we read it, believe it, and act upon the truth given to us. Jesus said in John 8:32, "And you shall know the truth, and the truth shall make you free."

Tombstone talk:
1. It's my fault.
2. What am I going to do? I have no place and no money.
3. I promise I will never do it again. I can't live without you.
4. I'll kill myself if you leave me. (Believe me, they won't.)
5. I know he loves me. He didn't mean it. (What did he mean?)
6. If it wasn't for the kids...
7. I must have done something because he's screaming so loud, and he is right because I can't remember, so I guess I am stupid, dumb, brainless.
8. Give me one more chance.
9. I know I'm seeing my family too much.
10. He told me my best friend wasn't really.
11. I should stay away from church.
12. What if my family and friends find out?
13. I talk too much. I better just keep quiet.
14. I hope he's in a good mood.
15. He likes to know where I am all the time.

Breaking the Curse of Abuse

After making a determination to leave, I stopped at my place of employment to get my paycheck and to turn in my notice. I rented a place for one month and was able to be alone with God to find out how this could be my fault. My first step of faith had been taken; I acted out what I had heard from God. All I had with me were a few clothes, my Bible, and my God, and that was all I needed. Proverbs 15:31 says, *"The ear that hears the rebukes of life will abide among the wise."* Wisdom is applying that knowledge, not just hearing it spoken. You must be teachable and obedient when God speaks. You must have a trust established with the words that the Lord speaks before you are able to act on them. God showed me, as I meditated on His Word, a scene with my family sitting at the dining room table. This was very familiar to me since we ate there every evening.

He showed me my position at the table as the submissive wife while my husband, at the head of the table, spoke negative words to each of us. The Holy Spirit asked, "Do I verbally abuse my children?" I said, "No." "Then why are you remaining silent while these words of death are spoken over your family? Do you not recall the scripture 'Death and life are in the power of the tongue and those who love it will eat its fruit'?" Deadly fruit was being served, and *I allowed it by keeping silent.* This was contrary to my counseling. I was taught that by being quiet and praying, God would then speak to my husband, who was the head of the family. God showed me that by keeping quiet, I had empowered and advanced the dark kingdom in my household. If we miss out on the whole counsel of God, then we only have a fraction of the truth.

The element necessary to provide *wholeness* is not there.

A confronter is a peacemaker.

God then explained the power of agreement. If we agree with His Word, it is already established in heaven, but if we agree with the enemy's word, it is established in his kingdom. He brought me back to those two kingdoms in the vision. He explained that when I agreed with His Word, I stayed in His kingdom, and I would hear from Him. When I came out of agreement with His Word and came into agreement with the enemy's words of death, I moved into the enemy's kingdom and could not hear from God. Sin separates us from the love of God, and He is jealous for our love. The seeds of death sown in my children and me were now growing into trees that were branching out. The Lord gave me Ephesians 5:11, *"And have no fellowship with the unfruitful works of darkness, but rather expose them."* Abuse is a curse that is passed down from the generations through an open door, and the open door is sin. I realized that I had sinned when I disobeyed Ephesians 5:11 and continued fellowshipping with abuse. I understood the picture God showed me on my knees with my hands up, worshiping Satan. Sin allows the operation of the abuse to continue in a family until it is exposed and stopped. We stop it by first confessing that we were in sin when we bowed our knees and served the demon of abuse. Through repentance, we are cleansed of sin, and by the blood of Jesus, we are restored into His kingdom. Sin separates us from God, and this is the reason why all those years, I was never able to hear the voice of the Lord in my abusive situation. What a revelation!

The Holy Spirit asked, "Is verbal abuse an unfruitful work of darkness?" I said, "Yes." He then asked, "Why then are you fellowshipping with it rather than exposing it?" He, the Holy Spirit, directed me to Ephesians 6:12 and showed me that we do not wrestle against flesh and blood but against principalities, against powers, against the rulers of darkness of this age and spiritual hosts of wickedness in heavenly places.

Your husband is not your enemy; you are battling the dark kingdom.

The enemy uses deception, intimidation, seduction, control, and fear with the abused victim. He wants you to believe there is no way out and that you deserve the abuse. *The truth* is there is a way out of abuse. You must guard your mouth from reacting to the abusive words, but rather calmly respond (respond, do not react!). Say, "I do not agree." When you speak these words, you have broken the agreement with the dark kingdom, and the words are now nullified and of no validity. The only way the enemy can place seeds within us is if we agree or keep silent. The devil cannot read your mind, he needs to hear a voice, and in order to expose him, you must name his name. You say, "I do not agree, this is verbal abuse, and I will no longer allow it." Now you have confronted the enemy (the devil) and not your husband or abuser.

In the Spirit realm (once named), he is now exposed, and once exposed, he loses his power. If the abuse does not stop, you are to remove yourself from the abuse. This can happen by saying, "I am going to leave the room, and later, we can discuss this." Once removed from the abuse, you must curse any deadly seeds that were spoken and command them to uproot from your life. If deadly words were spoken over your children, curse them and uproot them in Jesus' name. Words spoken over you or anyone, either in authority or otherwise, are potent, alive, and working. You must take every negative word and curse spoken against you and bring them to the cross and say, "Jesus, by your blood, I take every word ever spoken against me, and I cancel out the assignment." In the spirit realm, the demon's assignment has been stopped. *Praise the Lord!* If your children are too young, stand in the gap for them to break the words or curses off of them with the same prayer. If they are older, explain what those deadly words have done in their lives and ask them to pray this powerful prayer for release. A very important and vital step to take with your children, especially older ones who may have left home or who have experienced this deadly curse in their lives, is that you must go to them and ask forgiveness for allowing the abuse in your home. They were helpless victims who depended on you for safety, and there was none. You acted out of ignorance, but now you have the knowledge of the Lord, and you must speak it into their lives. This will be healing for everyone. Once again, the Lord told me that *I was never to stay in the presence of abuse.* Each situation will be different, depending on how long we have empowered and advanced the abuse in our home. Some husbands will follow you right into the next room and continue with abusive words. You just say, "I cannot stay around abuse. I am going to leave. When I come back later, perhaps we can discuss it." Remember your words, even in the heat of the moment, must be with *love.* This is where the quiet and gentle spirit is evident, and you have not reacted the same way as your abuser. The enemy was waiting for you to use your tongue to spew deadly seeds to the abuser. You would have been snared by the enemy and brought into his kingdom, but you have obeyed a powerful spiritual principle that will enable you to hear from God. God will give you wisdom on how to take the next step as long as you walk out this principle. As I obeyed these principles, the devil, by naming the name of abuse, lost his power, and God then empowered me. Now that demonic power is broken, and the real person (husband and/or abuser) has an opportunity to be convicted by the Lord.

You now become *God's freedom fighter. Always remove yourself from the presence of abuse.* Staying in God's kingdom allows the Lord to bring conviction to the abuser, never condemnation, because God created and loves the abuser, but not the abuse. Many times, verbal abuse is familiar because they grew up with it, and they don't know that it causes harm to both them and their families. When God's loving conviction comes, they realize the truth. A change can take place immediately; however, this must be borne out of fruit from your obeying these principles. If verbal abuse is permitted, it will escalate to physical abuse because the devil of abuse was empowered. God revealed this to me.

Physical abuse is a 911 call. Both abuser and victim are in the dark kingdom, and *God's authority is not in that household.* God established all authority on the earth, and when we call 911, we are bringing His established authority on this earth into our home. Once abuse is within the home, the authority is not. God has established His authority in the home through parents so they may raise godly offspring. God's authority is not in any household where there is abuse, and where abuse is allowed, both people, the abuser and the abused, are serving Satan. That is why God's outside established authority, the police, must be called in. The enemy will try every scheme to stop you from exposing him, but when you obey God and make that call, you will feel strength pour into your soul. God will give you the grace to walk through the situation. Abusers break the law and must be reported to the authorities, or Satan will continue to establish his rule there. The world's idea of love is a strong emotional attachment to another person.

It brings self-satisfaction and creates a sense of self-worth. We were all created by God with a need to be nurtured and loved. In an abusive home, the victim is starving for love, and the abuser has no love to give because they operate under demonic control. In most cases, after the abuse occurs, the abuser becomes fearful that the victim will tell on them and will try to quickly cover up the offense. They say things like, "It will never happen again, I promise," but if you do not make them accountable, the cycle will continue. You must understand what love is. Look at 1 Corinthians 13:4-8:

> Love suffers long and is kind; love does not envy; does not parade itself, is not puffed up; does not behave rudely, does not seek its own, is not provoked, thinks no evil, does not rejoice in iniquity, but rejoices in the truth; bears all things, believes all things, hopes all things, endures all things. Love never fails.

God's love is a selfless love and spiritual force that focuses on the needs of others before our own. You will clearly see that no love operates in an abusive home.

If you do not stop it, abuse will escalate to hospital visits, broken noses, bruises, burns on bodies, scarring, disabilities, and eventually, death. Yes, death. It will never stop until you stop it. Sexual abuse: When someone is sexually abusing you, this must be reported to the authorities. Sexual abuse can be operational within a married couple's life, and many times, a wife is raped. Yes, raped. This is not a consensual act when it is done with force and not with love. Seek the counsel of your pastor, and if this persists, you must follow the same principles that apply to abuse of any kind.

Name it, expose it, stop it! *Do not allow it!* If you are a parent and your child comes to you to expose a relative, friend of a family member, or stranger that has been sexually abusing them, you as the parent must listen and hear what they are saying. Let them know that you are there for their protection and safety, and tell them how glad you are that they confided in you. After verifying this, you must call the authorities. The abused victim may have to be removed from the home in order to begin the healing process, and they will need much prayer and deliverance. If sexual abuse is not exposed, the victim will continue to draw those with the same familiar spirit to them. They will usually become victims of rape, incest, and multiple sex partners. Shame, guilt, and condemnation will usually torment those sexually abused. They depend on you, the guardian that God has appointed over them, to protect them from harm. *The roadway to healing.* There is a wonderful roadway to healing for abuse victims. We need to stop the denial and be totally honest with our situation. *What you do not acknowledge, you can't change.* The beginning of peace is to stop the abuse. In John 8:3, Jesus took a stand against abuse when the religious leaders wanted to stone the woman caught in the act of adultery. He is grieved when He sees the enemy abusing His children. We are joint-heirs with Christ, and He wants us to live in righteousness, peace, and joy.

Repentance is the key to open the door to the kingdom of heaven and all the blessings. To open this door, you will need to repent for having allowed the sin of abuse. If you have taken an offense, repent of this. If you are holding unforgiveness, repent of it and then bless your abuser. You have now shut all doors where the operation of abuse was allowed to reign and allow the Lord to bring conviction and healing. You will now be able to hear His wisdom on the steps you need to take since there is no longer a separation through sin. Maybe you are the abuser and find yourself convicted after reading this message. There is hope for you; Jesus loves you, and He knows all about the abuse, and above all, He wants you healed and delivered from its horrible grip on your life. Pray this prayer with me, "Father, in the name of Jesus, I come to You asking for forgiveness for abusing (name them), and I ask that You wash me in the blood of Jesus Christ and cleanse me totally from abuse and all sin. I come out of agreement with the spirit of abuse and rebuke and command it to leave me now, in Jesus' name. I bless all those who I have abused and ask that You bring healing to their lives and to our relationships." If you have been abused, pray this prayer, "Father, in the name of Jesus, I come to you, repenting for allowing abuse in my life. Please, forgive me and wash me in the precious blood of Jesus Christ from all defilement. I forgive (name them), who abused me. I have come out of agreement with all abuse and will not allow it in my life again. I command the spirit of abuse to leave me now in Jesus' name. Thank You, Jesus, for setting me free. Amen." Please be sure to follow up with a mentor and pastor/counselor who will walk you through your roadway to healing.

The witness steps down.

"Remember: make no truce or excuse with abuse!"

—*Pepsi Freund*

The Judge Speaks His Verdict to the Abused & the Abuser

After carefully listening to all testimonies in this case, I have made a decision in this matter: I find both the Plaintiff (the abused) and the Defendant (the abuser) guilty as charged. Both have committed sin in this matter.

My witness: Theresa has revealed My truth to this court regarding the sin of abuse and its hold on one's life. By her testimony, the exact counsel I have declared to Theresa has now been declared to both the abuser and the abused. As the eternal Judge of this world, I have now equipped My chosen, whom I love, with these powerful truths on how to conduct your lives and how to overcome sin in your life.

My sentence: Learn these truths, declare them over your life daily until you know them "by heart," and teach them to your loved ones, for they are My personal counsel to you.

As an act of obedience to Your word, Lord, I (your name):

Do not enter the path of the wicked, and do not walk in the way of evil. Avoid it, do not travel on it; Turn away from it and pass on. For they do not sleep unless they have done evil; And their sleep is taken away unless they make someone fall. For they eat the bread of wickedness, and drink the wine of violence. But the path of the just is like the shining sun, that shines ever brighter unto the perfect day. The way of the wicked is like darkness; They do not know what makes them stumble. My son, give attention to my words; Incline your ear to my sayings.

Do not let them depart from your eyes; Keep them in the midst of your heart; For they are life to those who find them, and health to all their flesh. Keep your heart with all diligence, for out of it spring the issues of life. Put away from you a deceitful mouth, and put perverse lips far from you. Let your eyes look straight ahead, and your eyelids look right before you. Ponder the path of your feet, and let all your ways be established. Do not turn to the right or the left; Remove your foot from evil.

Proverbs 4:14-27

So Jesus said, "Are you also still without understanding? Do you not yet understand that whatever enters the mouth goes into the stomach and is eliminated? But those things which proceed out of the mouth come from the heart, and they defile a man. For out of the heart proceed evil thoughts, murders, adulteries, fornications, thefts, false witness, blasphemies. These are the things which defile a man, but to eat with unwashed hands does not defile a man."

Matthew 15:16-20

"Therefore, having these promises, beloved, let us cleanse ourselves from all filthiness of the flesh and spirit, perfecting holiness in the fear of God" (2 Corinthians 7:1).

Finally then, brethren, we urge and exhort in the Lord Jesus that you should abound more and more, just as you received from us how you ought to walk and to please God; for you know what commandments we gave you through the Lord Jesus. For this is the will of God, your sanctification: that you should abstain from sexual immorality; that each of you should know how to possess his own vessel in sanctification and honor, not in passion of lust, like the Gentiles who do not know God; that no one should take advantage of and defraud his brother in this matter, because the Lord is the avenger of all such, as we also forewarned you and testified. For God did not call us to uncleanness, but in holiness. Therefore he who rejects this does not reject man, but God, who has also given us His Holy Spirit.

1 Thessalonians 4:1-8

"And do not fear those who kill the body but cannot kill the soul. But rather fear Him who is able to destroy both soul and body in hell" (Matthew 10:28).

I beseech you therefore, brethren, by the mercies of God, that you present your bodies a living sacrifice, holy, acceptable to God, which is your reasonable service. And do not be conformed to this world, but be transformed by the renewing of your mind, that you may prove what is that good and acceptable and perfect will of God.

Romans 12:1-2

Blessed are the undefiled in the way, who walk in the law of the Lord! Blessed are those who keep His testimonies, who seek Him with the whole heart! They also do no iniquity; they walk in His ways. You have commanded us to keep Your precepts diligently. Oh, that my ways were directed to keep Your statutes! Then I would not be ashamed, When I look into all Your commandments. I will praise You with uprightness of heart, When I learn Your righteous judgments. I will keep Your statutes; Oh, do not forsake me utterly! How can a young man cleanse his way? By taking heed according to Your word. With my whole heart I have sought You; Oh, let me not wander from Your commandments! Your word I have hidden in my heart, That I might not sin against You. Blessed are You, O Lord! Teach me Your statutes. With my lips I have declared all the judgments of Your mouth. I have rejoiced in the way of Your testimonies, as much as in all riches. I will meditate on Your precepts, and contemplate Your ways. I will delight myself in Your statutes; I will not forget Your word.

Psalm 119:1-16

*Now this is the commandment, and these are the
statutes and judgments which the Lord your God
has commanded to teach you, that you may observe
them in the land which you are crossing over to possess, that you may fear the Lord your God, to keep
all His statutes and His commandments which I
command you, you and your son and your grand-
son, all the days of your life, and that your days
may be prolonged. Therefore hear, O Israel, and be
careful to observe it, that it may be well with you,
and that you may multiply greatly as the Lord God
of your fathers has promised you—'a land flowing
with milk and honey.' "Hear, O Israel: The Lord our
God, the Lord is one! You shall love the Lord your
God with all your heart, with all your soul, and
with all your strength.*

Deuteronomy 6:1-5

*"Do not be unequally yoked together with unbelievers. For
what fellowship has righteousness with lawlessness? And what
communion has light with darkness?"* (2 Corinthians 6:14)

God protects us from abuse:

*Have mercy on me, O Lord, for I am weak; O Lord,
heal me, for my bones are troubled. My soul also is
greatly troubled; But You, O Lord—how long? Re-*

*turn, O Lord, deliver me! Oh, save me for Your mer-
cies' sake! For in death there is no remembrance of
You; In the grave who will give You thanks? I am
weary with my groaning; All night I make my bed
swim; I drench my couch with my tears. My eye
wastes away because of grief; It grows old because
of all my enemies. Depart from me, all you workers
of iniquity; For the Lord has heard the voice of my
weeping. The Lord has heard my supplication; The
Lord will receive my prayer. Let all my enemies be
ashamed and greatly troubled; Let them turn back
and be ashamed suddenly.*

Psalm 6:2-10

*O Lord my God, in You I put my trust; Save me from
all those who persecute me; And deliver me, lest they
tear me like a lion, rending me in pieces, while there
is none to deliver. O Lord my God, if I have done this:
If there is iniquity in my hands, If I have repaid evil
to him who was at peace with me, or have plundered
my enemy without cause, Let the enemy pursue me
and overtake me; Yes, let him trample my life to the
earth, and lay my honor in the dust. Selah
Arise, O Lord, in Your anger; Lift Yourself up because of the rage of my enemies; Rise up for me to
the judgment You have commanded! So the congregation of the peoples shall surround You; For their*

125

sakes, therefore, return on high. The Lord shall judge the peoples; Judge me, O Lord, according to my righteousness, And according to my integrity within me. Oh, let the wickedness of the wicked come to an end, but establish the just; For the righteous God tests the hearts and minds. My defense is of God, who saves the upright in heart. God is a just judge, And God is angry with the wicked every day. If he does not turn back, He will sharpen His sword; He bends His bow and makes it ready. He also prepares for Himself instruments of death; He makes His arrows into fiery shafts. Behold, the wicked brings forth iniquity; Yes, he conceives trouble and brings forth falsehood. He made a pit and dug it out, and has fallen into the ditch which he made. His trouble shall return upon his own head, and his violent dealing shall come down on his own crown. I will praise the Lord according to His righteousness, and will sing praise to the name of the Lord Most High.

Psalm 7:1-17

A man of great wrath will suffer punishment; For if you rescue him, you will have to do it again. Listen to counsel and receive instruction, that you may be wise in your latter days. There are many plans in a man's heart, Nevertheless the Lord's counsel—that will stand. What is desired in a man is kindness, and a poor man is better than a liar. The fear of the Lord leads to life, and he who has it will abide in satisfaction; He will not be visited with evil.

Proverbs 19:19-23

"*For the Lord will pass through to strike the Egyptians; and when He sees the blood on the lintel and on the two doorposts, the Lord will pass over the door and not allow the destroyer to come into your houses to strike you*" (Exodus 12:23).

"*You shall not afflict any widow or fatherless child. If you afflict them in any way, and they cry at all to Me, I will surely hear their cry; and My wrath will become hot, and I will kill you with the sword; your wives shall be widows, and your children fatherless*" (Exodus 22:22-24).

Now early in the morning He came again into the temple, and all the people came to Him; and He sat down and taught them. Then the scribes and Pharisees brought to Him a woman caught in adultery. And when they had set her in the midst, they said to Him, "Teacher, this woman was caught in adultery, in the very act. Now Moses, in the law, commanded us that such should be stoned. But what do You say?" This they said, testing Him, that they might have something of which to accuse Him. But Jesus stooped down and wrote on the ground with His finger, as though He did not hear." So when they continued asking Him, He raised Himself up and said to them, "He who is without sin among you, let him throw a stone at her first."

And again He stooped down and wrote on the ground. Then those who heard it, being convicted by their conscience, went out one by one, beginning with the oldest even to the last. And Jesus was left alone, and the woman standing in the midst. When Jesus had raised Himself up and saw no one but the woman, He said to her, "Woman, where are those accusers of yours? Has no one condemned you?" She said, "No one, Lord." And Jesus said to her, Neither do I condemn you; go and sin no more.

John 8:2-11

In the Lord I put my trust; How can you say to my soul, "Flee as a bird to your mountain"? For look! The wicked bend their bow, they make ready their arrow on the string, that they may shoot secretly at the upright in heart. If the foundations are destroyed, What can the righteous do? The Lord is in His holy temple, The Lord's throne is in heaven; His eyes behold, His eyelids test the sons of men. The Lord tests the righteous, But the wicked and the one who loves violence His soul hates. Upon the wicked

He will rain coals; Fire and brimstone and a burning wind shall be the portion of their cup. For the Lord is righteous, He loves righteousness; His countenance beholds the upright.

Psalm 11:1-7

Do not be deceived, God is not mocked; for whatever a man sows, that he will also reap. For he who sows to his flesh will of the flesh reap corruption, but he who sows to the Spirit will of the Spirit reap everlasting life. And let us not grow weary while doing good, for in due season we shall reap if we do not lose heart. Therefore, as we have opportunity, let us do good to all, especially to those who are of the household of faith.

Galatians 6:7-10

A *true story*: Many years ago, I met a woman named Darlene (not her real name) at a local church who was a very powerful prayer warrior. We immediately became friends as I loved to pray as well. I was a young believer at the time. The incredible wisdom she walked in regarding the Word of God was fascinating to me. We prayed together at our local church, and one day, she opened up to me to share something very troubling about her home life. She and her husband moved to Florida from another country. She became a believer in Christ years after they were married. She was so completely changed by reading God's Word daily and had a great hunger to draw as close to the Lord as possible.

Well, her husband was very different, and his attitude toward her after her conversion was negative, and she told him that he needed to ask Jesus into his heart, and he would be a changed person. He became enraged with her and stated she could not and better not mention that name again to him. She was in shock, to say the least. She went on daily reading her Bible when one day, he walked in the door and screamed at her saying, "Put that book away. I want it out of my sight." She ran to her room in tears, and as she prayed, he said, "Shut up, I don't want to hear you at all." I prayed with her, and we agreed God would stop this horrible abuse.

I felt so bad for her. I tried to see if there was an affordable building that we could rent and have prayer regularly. That wasn't in the Lord's plan as I moved away about four months later. This chilling story came to an end when I met her again about a year later at a meeting while visiting family. She told me that God answered our prayers one day just as He did in the book of Ezekiel 9:1-11. I wasn't familiar with this scripture, but after reading it, I didn't understand what she meant. She said, "The abuse got worse, and he followed me everywhere I went to make sure I wasn't praying or reading my Bible." One day he got home early, and she had her Bible in her hand. He caught her, and he went and got a knife and chased her with it to murder her. She went into the bathroom to be safe, and he kicked open the door. Standing there with the knife in position to attack her, she cried, "Lord, help me, please!" She said there was something or someone there holding him back from her. She knew it was an angel of the Lord. She said he kept trying to push past it to kill her, but he was unable to move forward. Just then, he dropped to the floor and died.

He had a massive heart attack, and she called an ambulance, but he died instantly. I will never forget that story. This is a sobering warning found in the Word regarding God's protection: *"Do not touch My anointed ones, and do My prophets no harm"* (Psalm 105:15).

We are in the last days: We are truly beginning to see the Bible unfolding before our eyes today as we hear reports of earthquakes, pestilences, and rumors of wars. We have never seen such an increase in events happen so quickly around us. I want to share with you a word the Lord released to me back in January of 2016.

Word of the Lord given to Diane Bernardin on January 2, 2016: "For I am about to bring a whirlwind in epidemic proportions (widespread) to this world. For they are about to see My mighty hand displayed to shift and change governments, and many regions will collapse under the weight of My mighty right hand. For kings will bow down before Me; they will cry out to Me to come and save and rescue them. I will cause a great shaking, but it will bring the great awakening of My Spirit all across the land. For the earth shall be filled with the knowledge of the glory of My presence. Kings will run to and fro looking for help from other nations, but I will be the only help they find.

"2 Chronicles 7:14: *'If My people who are called by My name will humble themselves, and pray and seek My face, and turn from their wicked ways, then I will hear from heaven, and will forgive their sin and heal their land.'* For I am about to display My beauty to My bride in magnificent ways. For My bride has sought after Me, she has followed My ways, and her heart is turned fully toward Me. I will be exalted in the universe, and My kingdom will rule and reign on planet earth. Multitudes, multitudes in the valley of decision, seeking their own ways, serving false gods, but I, the Lord of glory, will gather together those that are Mine. Those whose hearts are fully Mine. The time of the gathering of My harvest is coming; be ready!"

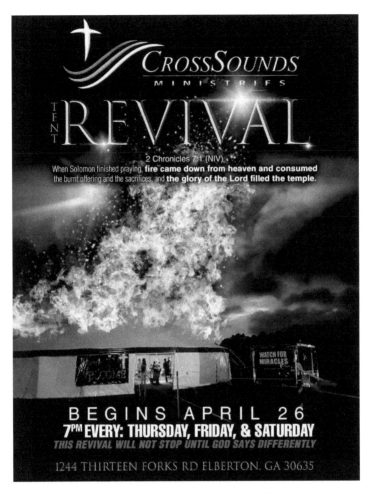

CrossSounds Ministries Gospel Tent

Vision given to Diane Bernardin March 3, 2018: While in prayer for a gospel tent meeting we were having in April 2018, I saw a massive flow of fire coming from heaven toward the earth with rippling waves that moved as if they were living. As it came toward the gos-

pel tent that was up, I knew in my spirit that the Lord
sent the fire, and He spoke to my heart that this fire
would consume all that defiled. Malachi 3:1-3.

On February 15th, 2019, this word also was given to
me, so I include it with this vision from 2018: "For I am
about to bring My people into a place of a fiery furnace
where I will burn out the chaff. I will burn out the bond-
age they have been holding onto for years. And when
they are refined, I will pull them out and rescue them,
and I will pour My oil upon them and use them to set
the captives free."

*"And you shall take the anointing oil, pour it on his head,
and anoint him"* (Exodus 29:7).

*"When Solomon finished praying, fire flashed down from
heaven and burned up the burnt offerings and sacrifices,
and the glorious presence of the LORD filled the Temple"* (2
Chronicles 7:1).

*"John answered, saying to all, 'I indeed baptize you with
water; but One mightier than I is coming, whose sandal strap
I am not worthy to loose. He will baptize you with the Holy
Spirit and fire'"* (Luke 3:16).

Acts 4:23-35 lists the following signs that revealed a
great awakening:

> *And being let go, they went to their own companions
> and reported all that the chief priests and elders had
> said to them. So when they heard that, they raised*

their voice to God with one accord and said: "Lord, You are God, who made heaven and earth and the sea, and all that is in them, who by the mouth of Your servant David have said: 'Why did the nations rage, And the people plot vain things? The kings of the earth took their stand, And the rulers were gathered together Against the LORD and against His Christ.' For truly against Your holy Servant Jesus, whom You anointed, both Herod and Pontius Pilate, with the Gentiles and the people of Israel, were gathered together to do whatever Your hand and Your purpose determined before to be done. Now, Lord, look on their threats, and grant to Your servants that with all boldness they may speak Your word, by stretching out Your hand to heal, and that signs and wonders may be done through the name of Your holy Servant Jesus." And when they had prayed, the place where they were assembled together was shaken; and they were all filled with the Holy Spirit, and they spoke the word of God with boldness. Now the multitude of those who believed were of one heart and one soul; neither did anyone say that any of the things he possessed was his own, but they had all things in common. And with great power the apostles gave witness to the resurrection of the Lord Jesus. And great grace was upon them all. Nor was there anyone among them who lacked;

for all who were possessors of lands or houses sold them, and brought the proceeds of the things that were sold, and laid them at the apostles' feet; and they distributed to each as anyone had need.

1. Miracles following the word believed.
2. Boldness when opposed.
3. Prayer bringing shaking and baptism in the Holy Spirit.
4. Believers are multiplied and are in unity in heart and soul.
5. Great power and great grace upon all who witness.
6. All needs are supplied, no lack.

Finally, all of you be of one mind, having compassion for one another; love as brothers, be tenderhearted, be courteous; not returning evil for evil or reviling for reviling, but on the contrary blessing, knowing that you were called to this, that you may inherit a blessing. For "He who would love life and see good days, let him refrain his tongue from evil, and his lips from speaking deceit. Let him turn away from evil and do good; Let him seek peace and pursue it. For the eyes of the Lord are on the righteous, and His ears are open to their prayers; But the face of the Lord is against those who do evil."

And who is he who will harm you if you become fol-
lowers of what is good? But even if you should suf-
fer for righteousness' sake, you are blessed. "And do
not be afraid of their threats, nor be troubled." But
sanctify the Lord God in your hearts, and always
be ready to give a defense to everyone who asks you
a reason for the hope that is in you, with meekness
and fear; having a good conscience, that when they
defame you as evildoers, those who revile your good
conduct in Christ may be ashamed. For it is better,
if it is the will of God, to suffer for doing good than
for doing evil.

1 Peter 3:8-17

We have hope and an inheritance:

Blessed be the God and Father of our Lord Jesus
Christ, who according to His abundant mercy has
begotten us again to a living hope through the res-
urrection of Jesus Christ from the dead, to an in-
heritance incorruptible and undefiled and that does
not fade away, reserved in heaven for you, who are
kept by the power of God through faith for salva-
tion ready to be revealed in the last time. In this you
greatly rejoice, though now for a little while, if need
be, you have been grieved by various trials, that the
genuineness of your faith, being much more pre-

cious than gold that perishes, though it is tested by fire, may be found to praise, honor, and glory at the revelation of Jesus Christ, whom having not seen you love.

Though now you do not see Him, yet believing, you rejoice with joy inexpressible and full of glory, receiving the end of your faith—the salvation of your souls. Of this salvation the prophets have inquired and searched carefully, who prophesied of the grace that would come to you, searching what, or what manner of time, the Spirit of Christ who was in them was indicating when He testified beforehand the sufferings of Christ and the glories that would follow. To them it was revealed that, not to themselves, but to us they were ministering the things which now have been reported to you through those who have preached the gospel to you by the Holy Spirit sent from heaven—things which angels desire to look into. Therefore gird up the loins of your mind, be sober, and rest your hope fully upon the grace that is to be brought to you at the revelation of Jesus Christ; as obedient children, not conforming yourselves to the former lusts, as in your ignorance; but as He who called you is holy, you also be holy in all your conduct, because it is written, "Be holy, for I am holy."

1 Peter 1:3-16

"If you judge people, you have no time to love them."

Mother Theresa

CHAPTER 13

Win the Lost

We are all called to be ministers of reconciliation.

Now all things are of God, who has reconciled us to himself through Jesus Christ, and has given us the ministry of reconciliation, That is, that God was in Christ, reconciling the world to Himself, not imputing their trespasses to them, and has committed to us the word of reconciliation. Now then, we are ambassadors for Christ, as though God were pleading through us: we implore you on Christ's behalf, be reconciled to God.

2 Corinthians 5:18-20

An ambassador of a kingdom represents the kingdom that he dwells in. He is fully permitted to speak on behalf of his king. There are many Christians today who faithfully go to church every Sunday and listen to their pastor preach and give an invitation to the lost to turn their lives over to Jesus Christ. They leave the ministry to the pastor only; they go home and do nothing for the Lord.

We have a commission from the Lord Jesus as His disciples:

> *And He said unto them, 'Go into all the world, and preach the gospel to every creature. He who believes and is baptized will be saved; but he who does not believe will be condemned. And these signs will follow those who believe: In My name they will cast out demons; they will speak with new tongues; They will take up serpents; and if they drink anything deadly, it will by no means hurt them; they will lay hands on sick, and they will recover.' So then after the Lord had spoken to them, He was received up into heaven, and sat down at the right hand of God. And they went out, and preached everywhere, the Lord working with them, and confirming the word through the accompanying signs. Amen.*
>
> Mark 16:15-20

Any saint who is born again can win another person to Christ. You only need to be willing to share with others your testimony as the Lord draws people to you. The most important thing you can do is listen to the person and allow the Lord to show you their need. Share His wonderful love with them and share how Jesus changed your life after you were saved. We all have a powerful testimony. Offer to pray with them to receive Christ. A simple prayer from the heart to Him is all that is needed. "Father, in the name of Jesus, I confess to You that I am a sinner in need of a Savior. Thank You for giving Your only Son, Jesus, who shed His blood and died for my sins on a cross, so that I would be forgiven and have eternal life. I ask for forgiveness for all my sins, and I choose to forgive all those who have sinned against me. Lord Jesus, please come live in me and bring change to my life. Fill me with Your Holy Spirit and empower me to walk and live a Christian life. Thank You, Father, in Jesus' name, amen." Then, pray for the Holy Spirit to fill them up with His presence just as on the day of Pentecost. Read Acts Chapter 2. Jesus said it is for our benefit that He went away because He would pray to the Father and ask Him to send us the comforter, the Holy Spirit who would live inside of us. He said He would not leave us as orphans (John 14:16-18).

Be filled with the Holy Spirit, and you will be empowered to be witnesses as His ambassadors in the kingdom of God. We need the Holy Spirit to empower us to walk the Christian walk in truth and be able to resist the enemy and his temptations to sin. Just simply ask Jesus to release the Holy Spirit to you and receive Him. "Fill this brother/sister up with the overflowing power and person of the Holy Spirit, Father, I pray, in

Jesus' name. Out of their belly shall flow rivers of living water, You said. Thank You for hearing and answering our prayer Lord, amen."

"My little children, let us not love in word, neither in tongue; but in deed and in truth."

Unknown

CHAPTER 14

Release His Great Love

The greatest truth of this entire book is this: love never fails. This is the one promise the Word of God says will work every time, in every situation you will ever face in this life. *"Hatred stirs up strife: but love covers all sins"* (Proverbs 10:12). *"He that loves not knows not God, for God is love"* (1 John 4:8). I have personally watched the love of Jesus melt the coldest of hearts. Love is the most powerful force you will ever contain within, and without any doubt, it is what every human being on this earth has a need of. I will never forget these wonderful testimonies I am about to share with you, as they changed Michel and my life forever, as well as the special people we simply reached out to along our journey.

I remember many years ago, Phillip from Florida, who was raised to believe in reincarnation, befriended my two young daughters and began to share with them his false doctrine, which was causing much confusion.

One morning, after prayer, I was leaving my apartment when I saw Phillip standing outside in his yard, and I was immediately angry inside. I really wanted to tell him off for trying to confuse my girls when the Lord interrupted me. He spoke to my heart, "Diane, tell Phillip that I love him."

Well, I argued, "Lord, you see how that kid is trying to cause trouble with my girls." Again, those words came to me, "Diane, tell Phillip that I love him." Well, reluctantly, I shouted over, "Hey, Phillip, do you know that Jesus loves you?" Just afterward, the Lord opened my spiritual eyes to see an incredible vision of gushing water coming from my belly area (like a fire hydrant cap pulled off), and it flowed across the yard to Philip's heart. I was amazed and asked, "Lord, what is this I am seeing?" The Lord answered, "Diane, it is not your love that Phillip needs, but it is My love that Phillip needs." *"Now hope does not disappoint, because the love of God has been poured out in our hearts by the Holy Spirit who was given to us"* (Romans 5:5).

The Lord revealed the great powerful love that He has for us through that vision. The love of God is what we truly need. You can see how many try to fill the empty places in their soul with counterfeit things that can never satisfy (drugs, alcohol, and food, to name a few). *"He who believes in me, as the scripture has said, out of his heart will flow rivers of living water. But this He spoke con-*

cerning the Spirit, whom those believing on him would receive: for the Holy Spirit was not yet given; because that Jesus was not yet glorified" (John 7:38-39).

Well, later that day, the girls and I went to the pool for a swim, and Phillip showed up. The Lord caused him to ask questions, and before long, I was leading Phillip to Jesus as Lord and Savior. The Lord asked me to baptize him in the swimming pool, and I said, "Lord, I can't baptize him; I'm not a minister." Well, the Lord told me a second time, and I baptized Phillip in water in the swimming pool, and the presence of God was strong. Phillip was on the heart of the Lord to get saved and be water baptized. He was a very grateful and very changed young man. I was so grateful that the Lord loved Phillip so much and used me as His mouthpiece that day.

I remember one night, late when Michel and I were so tired and wanted to get a motel room. When we met the front desk clerk, he was from the same state that I was from. While we shared some info and signed in, the Lord prompted me to ask him where he went to church. He said he didn't go anywhere, so I asked him if he knew Jesus as his Lord, and he said no, but he would like to. I told him how much the Lord loved him and sent us there to tell him about His great love for him. I told him how he had a divine purpose here on this earth, but in order to know what that purpose was, he must first be introduced to the God who made him. He said, "Yes, please pray with me. I want to know God." I led him to Jesus Christ right there. The total conversation time with him was about ten minutes. To God be the praise!

Next, Michel and I went into this store one night, and there was a young girl behind the register that we were drawn to. I could see how hurt she was. They had a restaurant connected to the store, so we decided to grab something to eat. The same girl walked into the restaurant, and I mentioned her to Michel, and he agreed she needed prayer, but he said, "Wait till we are ready to leave, and we will go talk to her." On the way out, she rang up our bill, and Michel began to share with her what the Lord had shown him about her, and she began to cry, asking how he knew that about her.

We shared the love of Christ with her, and Michel said, "It is time to turn your life over to Him," and we led her to Jesus right there in a check-out line. She was so grateful we took that time with her. As these prophetic words are released, they are very similar to scripture when Jesus met the Samaritan woman at the well. Jesus told her all about her current and former relationships through a word of knowledge. He knew all about her and didn't judge her but offered her living water (John 4:7-26).

These encounters were just like that, and all we had to do was become available when the Lord wanted us to minister, putting aside our agendas for heaven's agenda. There was a church that Michel and I attended on Christmas Eve, and the pastor called us up to pray for us. The Lord told him to take up an offering for us, and they collected $62.00. We were astonished that the Lord would desire to bless us like that so unexpectedly.

Well, the Lord spoke to Michel to use the money to buy a desk for his office, so we began searching all over for one reasonably priced. He found a desk that would work perfectly, and we drove quite a ways away to get it. We met this precious woman who looked like she had been in a terrible battle. We spoke to her briefly the first visit but told her that we would be back to pick up the desk in a few weeks. When we came back, I had a chance to sit with her in her living room, and within minutes, the Lord's presence began to fill that room. She had gone through some terrible abuse in a relationship, and it looked like the devil used this person to literally try to kill her.

She was so grateful to hear we were Christians, and after Michel loaded the truck with the desk, we both began to pray for deliverance for her. She was crying so hard, and the Lord set her totally free. She was so hopeless, so lifeless when we arrived there, but after the Lord loved her, we knew that she was a divinely ordered heavenly appointment who needed to be filled with the hope and love of the Lord Jesus. She called us a few weeks after we left, saying how many things had turned around for her. We were all so grateful for meeting and for the Lord meeting the need for that desk! What He won't do to make sure our steps are divinely ordered to be at heaven's right place at the right time, to fulfill heaven's purpose over these lives and others.

Michel and I sold furniture at a small store, and one of the items was a beautiful wooden entertainment center. Well, because of the new flat-screen TVs, it was hard to find a buyer. We prayed, and the Lord sent this precious Christian woman who came three times. We were told to measure the opening for the TV. Well, she bought it, and we were asked to deliver it to her at her home. She said that her son gave her a television years ago, and she had looked everywhere to find the most perfect fit. We were so blessed to have what she needed. As the night went on, we could sense the presence of the Lord increasing, so we stayed to encourage her and pray for her, and we had a revival in that place!

The Lord moved prophetically upon Michel and me, and we confirmed some things she had prayed about that very day. Thanks be to You, Lord, to see how much You care about our business and bring answers to the things that concern Your people. What a God of love! We wanted to attend a Spirit-filled church and see if that was where the Lord would plant us in our local area. During the service, a young woman went up to the altar area to get a tissue. The Holy Spirit drew me to her. I wanted to go to her and pray for her, but I didn't feel it was the right time. After service, I prayed that the Lord would bring her to me if He wanted me to pray for her. I turned around after speaking to someone, and there she was before me. I really felt the Lord wanted me to encourage her. She began to weep as I prayed for her, telling her what the Lord laid on my heart for her. Michel was encouraging another woman, and we prayed for her, and the Lord set her free from some things tormenting her. Then, the other woman I prayed for came over to us again, and Michel had the word of the Lord for her, and she began to shake and fall to the ground. Jesus set that precious woman free from years of abuse and shame in just a few minutes of time. Glory to His all-powerful name and yoke-destroying anointing!

His love is so rich for you and me, and it far exceeds any love that we know here on this earth. His love is unconditional and is always available to you whenever you call upon His wonderful name, Jesus. He is always there.

Now, I would like to pray for you. Heavenly Father, in Jesus' mighty name, I pray for you, precious saint:

That Christ may dwell in your hearts through faith; that you, being rooted and grounded in love, may be able to comprehend with all saints what is the width and length and depth and height, to know the love of Christ, which passes knowledge, that you may be filled with all the fullness of God. Now to Him who is able to do exceedingly abundantly above all that we ask or think, according to the power that works in us, to him be glory in the church by Christ Jesus to all generations, forever and ever. Amen.

Ephesians 3:17-21

In Conclusion

In conclusion, I would exhort you to always walk in His love, His mercy, His amazing grace, and true forgiveness toward others at all times. Guard your hearts against all offenses that come toward you, and do not allow them to remain. Remember the cross He carried for you and how much He suffered for your salvation and healing. Share His unconditional love with others He brings your way. Encourage others in the faith and pray for one another always.

Tell someone about your wonderful Savior and win them over to Him. Draw closer to Him daily through His word and prayer, and don't forget to worship Him from your heart. Pray in the Spirit continuously and pray with your understanding from a pure and undivided heart. In every circumstance, praise Him and thank Him for the victory in the outcome. If you have never met my Savior Jesus, now is the perfect time to meet Him. He longs for a relationship with you and is longing to meet you too. He came to this earth long ago to introduce His Father's kingdom.

He suffered horribly and died on a cross two thousand years ago for your sins and mine. He willingly gave up His precious life in exchange for you to know Him. He paid the penalty of death for sin that you and I should have paid, all because of His unending love for us. His precious blood was poured over a mercy seat for you in heaven, making full payment.

You only need to surrender your life to Him and be willing to put your hand into His and allow Him to lead you and guide you through this life. He knows the plans for your life already, and He desires to show them to you each day of your life. He is so kind and gentle and desires you to experience His personal touch in your life. He died on the cross for your sins, past, present, and future. He promises to never leave you nor forsake you and will be with you until the end of the age.

Would you like to invite Him into your heart and be His forever? The Bible says all have sinned and fall short of the glory of God, so there is one thing we all have in common. The good news is that *"For He made Him who knew no sin to be sin for us, that we might become the righteousness of God in Him"* (2 Corinthians 5:21), and even while we were yet sinners, Christ died for us. You don't have to qualify or be good enough to come to Him. You need to come just as you are.

Pray out loud with me: "Father, I thank You for loving me so much that You gave Your only Son Jesus to die on the cross for my sins. Lord Jesus, I need You so desperately in my life. I am so thankful that You went to the cross for my sins. Lord, I am asking You to please forgive me for every sin I have ever committed, and please wash me in Your precious blood from all unrighteousness. I choose to forgive every person who sinned against me. Please fill me with Your Holy Spirit so I can live in your presence and grow in knowledge daily. Thank You, Lord, for coming in. I commit myself to live for You and serve You all the days of my life."

I pray: "Father, bless this precious saint for the commitment they made to You. I thank You that their name has been added to the Lamb's Book of Life in heaven. Thank You that all of heaven is rejoicing over this beautiful surrender to You, Lord. Fill them up with the Holy Spirit, I pray right now, and manifest Your presence to them and make them Your witnesses." I welcome you to the family of God. You are now my brother or sister in Christ!

May His peace remain upon you all the days of your life, and may His presence be in you, around you, and flow through you always.

"Lord, grant that I might not so much seek to be loved as to love."

St. Francis of Assisi

Contact
Information

Contact me: CrossSounds Ministries

www.crosssounds.org

Diane@crosssounds.org

About the Author

Diane and her husband, Michel, are residents of Elberton, Georgia. Diane was born in Illinois and born again in 1984 and was a long-term member of the Rock of Sarasota, Florida, under the covering of Pastor Richard Brantley for nine years. She served in the Children's Ministry, Singles Ministry, and Set Free Ministries, as well as the Healing Rooms.

She also served as vice president of the Sarasota Chapter of Women's Aglow in 2001 and five years served as vice president of outreach in local Elberton Aglow. Diane is a graduate of Ethnoslink International Ministry Training Center in 2001 and received an associate's degree. She has authored several books.

Michel and Diane lead CrossSounds Ministries in Elberton, Georgia, and are active in the communities through street ministry outreaches with training, equipping, and prayer rallies. They have two grown children and three grandchildren.

About Theresa

Theresa Duffy was born and raised in New York City. She is the mother of three grown children and was born again in 1979 and moved at the same time to Florida.

Theresa was a founding member of the Rock of Sarasota Church under the covering of Pastor Richard Brantley for over twelve years. She has served in Singles Ministry as well as Set Free Ministries. Theresa is a graduate of the Christian Retreat Institute of Ministry. She has spoken at several Women's Aglow meetings and area churches. She is the leader of a Prophetic Intercessors prayer group as well as a mentor in the body of Christ.